ISBN 0-8373-0619-1

C-619   CAREER EXAMINATION SERIES

This is your
PASSBOOK® for...

Probation Officer

Test Preparation Study Guide

Questions & Answers

NLC

NATIONAL LEARNING CORPORATION

PASSBOOK®

NOTICE

This book is SOLELY intended for, is sold ONLY to, and its use is RESTRICTED to *individual*, bona fide applicants or candidates who qualify by virtue of having seriously filed applications for appropriate license, certificate, professional and/or promotional advancement, higher school matriculation, scholarship, or other legitimate requirements of educational and/or governmental authorities.

This book is NOT intended for use, class instruction, tutoring, training, duplication, copying, reprinting, excerption, or adaptation, etc., by:

(1) Other publishers

(2) Proprietors and/or Instructors of "Coaching" and/or Preparatory Courses

(3) Personnel and/or Training Divisions of commercial, industrial, and governmental organizations

(4) Schools, colleges, or universities and/or their departments and staffs, including teachers and other personnel

(5) Testing Agencies or Bureaus

(6) Study groups which seek by the purchase of a single volume to copy and/or duplicate and/or adapt this material for use by the group as a whole without having purchased individual volumes for each of the members of the group

(7) Et al.

Such persons would be in violation of appropriate Federal and State statutes.

PROVISION OF LICENSING AGREEMENTS. — Recognized educational commercial, industrial, and governmental institutions and organizations, and others legitimately engaged in educational pursuits, including training, testing, and measurement activities, may address a request for a licensing agreement to the copyright owners, who will determine whether, and under what conditions, including fees and charges, the materials in this book may be used by them. In other words, a licensing facility exists for the legitimate use of the material in this book on other than an individual basis. However, it is asseverated and affirmed here that the material in this book *CANNOT* be used without the receipt of the express permission of such a licensing agreement from the Publishers.

NATIONAL LEARNING CORPORATION
212 Michael Drive
Syosset, New York 11791

Inquiries re licensing agreements should be addressed to:
The President
National Learning Corporation
212 Michael Drive
Syosset, New York 11791

PASSBOOK® SERIES

THE *PASSBOOK® SERIES* has been created to prepare applicants and candidates for the ultimate academic battlefield – the examination room.

At some time in our lives, each and every one of us may be required to take an examination – for validation, matriculation, admission, qualification, registration, certification, or licensure.

Based on the assumption that every applicant or candidate has met the basic formal educational standards, has taken the required number of courses, and read the necessary texts, the *PASSBOOK® SERIES* furnishes the one special preparation which may assure passing with confidence, instead of failing with insecurity. Examination questions – together with answers – are furnished as the basic vehicle for study so that the mysteries of the examination and its compounding difficulties may be eliminated or diminished by a sure method.

This book is meant to help you pass your examination provided that you qualify and are serious in your objective.

The entire field is reviewed through the huge store of content information which is succinctly presented through a provocative and challenging approach – the question-and-answer method.

A climate of success is established by furnishing the correct answers at the end of each test.

You soon learn to recognize types of questions, forms of questions, and patterns of questioning. You may even begin to anticipate expected outcomes.

You perceive that many questions are repeated or adapted so that you can gain acute insights, which may enable you to score many sure points.

You learn how to confront new questions, or types of questions, and to attack them confidently and work out the correct answers.

You note objectives and emphases, and recognize pitfalls and dangers, so that you may make positive educational adjustments.

Moreover, you are kept fully informed in relation to new concepts, methods, practices, and directions in the field.

You discover that you are actually taking the examination all the time: you are preparing for the examination by "taking" an examination, not by reading extraneous and/or supererogatory textbooks.

In short, this PASSBOOK®, used directedly, should be an important factor in helping you to pass your test.

PROBATION OFFICER

DUTIES
The Probation Officer is the beginning position at the professional level in probation work. The duties require the application of modern social work techniques in making evaluations of adults to juveniles and in supervising persons on probation. A Probation Officer is called upon to exercise sound professional judgment in analyzing data and making recommendations concerning court dispositions. A Probation Officer works under the supervision of a higher ranking professional employee and may help to supervise the work of Probation Assistants, Probation Officer Trainees, or volunteers.

JOB DESCRIPTION
Under supervision, with some latitude for independent or unreviewed action or decision, performs work of varying degrees of difficulty and responsibility in probation, providing services for assigned individuals in intake, investigation, supervision and enforcement; performs related work.

EXAMPLES OF TYPICAL TASKS
Makes preliminary investigations of crimes or offenses, covering such matters as the nature of the offense, the place and manner in which it was committed, the circumstances, and the statements of the complainant and defendant. Obtains information on the offender's legal, economic, and psycho-social history and background. Makes initial and supervising investigations of cases involving family problems, such as neglect, child abuse, adoption, and non-support; enforces payments of fines, restitutions, and reparations ordered by the court. Clarifies information and answers questions for assigned individuals; prepares and submits written reports and recommendations, including revocation of probation if necessary. Keeps track of court cases in which the department is involved. Refers probationers to social, governmental or community agencies, or other entities which may assist in probationer's rehabilitation; performs field work which includes home visits to individuals under investigation or supervision; corresponds with and makes collateral visits to friends, relatives, community agencies, employers, former employers, churches, schools, law enforcement agencies, and others. Prepares and maintains case records. Serves as department representative as may be required. May supervise assigned personnel and volunteers. Acts as liaison between the department and the courts. Provides specialized services in identified programs which support the various operational services of the Department. Provides intake services to determine the necessity for court intervention or adjusts matters without referral to court. Provides supervision to case loads of probationers. Supervises caseloads of specially identified substance abusing probationers. When assigned to the Field Services Unit, performs violation of probation warrant investigations; makes collateral field visits; enforces violation of probation warrants; executes warrants; performs" failure to report" investigations and requisite field visits; detains or takes into custody probationers wanted by law enforcement agencies; assists in the preparation of cases for the Violation of Probation process; and executes search warrants. Conducts field visits and "failure to report" investigations of probationers. Conducts field visits, surveillances, and crisis intervention. Supervises caseloads of individuals conditionally released from local jails.

SCOPE OF EXAMINATION
The written test will be designed to test for knowledge, skills and/or abilities in such areas as: establishing and maintaining working relationships with defendants/respondents and probationers; and preparing written material, which may include written comprehension, written expression, memorization, problem sensitivity, deductive reasoning, and information ordering.

———

HOW TO TAKE A TEST

I. YOU MUST PASS AN EXAMINATION

A. *WHAT EVERY CANDIDATE SHOULD KNOW*

Examination applicants often ask us for help in preparing for the written test. What can I study in advance? What kinds of questions will be asked? How will the test be given? How will the papers be graded?

As an applicant for a civil service examination, you may be wondering about some of these things. Our purpose here is to suggest effective methods of advance study and to describe civil service examinations.

Your chances for success on this examination can be increased if you know how to prepare. Those "pre-examination jitters" can be reduced if you know what to expect. You can even experience an adventure in good citizenship if you know why civil service exams are given.

B. *WHY ARE CIVIL SERVICE EXAMINATIONS GIVEN?*

Civil service examinations are important to you in two ways. As a citizen, you want public jobs filled by employees who know how to do their work. As a job seeker, you want a fair chance to compete for that job on an equal footing with other candidates. The best-known means of accomplishing this two-fold goal is the competitive examination.

Exams are widely publicized throughout the nation. They may be administered for jobs in federal, state, city, municipal, town or village governments or agencies.

Any citizen may apply, with some limitations, such as the age or residence of applicants. Your experience and education may be reviewed to see whether you meet the requirements for the particular examination. When these requirements exist, they are reasonable and applied consistently to all applicants. Thus, a competitive examination may cause you some uneasiness now, but it is your privilege and safeguard.

C. *HOW ARE CIVIL SERVICE EXAMS DEVELOPED?*

Examinations are carefully written by trained technicians who are specialists in the field known as "psychological measurement," in consultation with recognized authorities in the field of work that the test will cover. These experts recommend the subject matter areas or skills to be tested; only those knowledges or skills important to your success on the job are included. The most reliable books and source materials available are used as references. Together, the experts and technicians judge the difficulty level of the questions.

Test technicians know how to phrase questions so that the problem is clearly stated. Their ethics do not permit "trick" or "catch" questions. Questions may have been tried out on sample groups, or subjected to statistical analysis, to determine their usefulness.

Written tests are often used in combination with performance tests, ratings of training and experience, and oral interviews. All of these measures combine to form the best-known means of finding the right person for the right job.

II. HOW TO PASS THE WRITTEN TEST

A. NATURE OF THE EXAMINATION

To prepare intelligently for civil service examinations, you should know how they differ from school examinations you have taken. In school you were assigned certain definite pages to read or subjects to cover. The examination questions were quite detailed and usually emphasized memory. Civil service exams, on the other hand, try to discover your present ability to perform the duties of a position, plus your potentiality to learn these duties. In other words, a civil service exam attempts to predict how successful you will be. Questions cover such a broad area that they cannot be as minute and detailed as school exam questions.

In the public service similar kinds of work, or positions, are grouped together in one "class." This process is known as *position-classification*. All the positions in a class are paid according to the salary range for that class. One class title covers all of these positions, and they are all tested by the same examination.

B. FOUR BASIC STEPS

1) Study the announcement

How, then, can you know what subjects to study? Our best answer is: "Learn as much as possible about the class of positions for which you've applied." The exam will test the knowledge, skills and abilities needed to do the work.

Your most valuable source of information about the position you want is the official exam announcement. This announcement lists the training and experience qualifications. Check these standards and apply only if you come reasonably close to meeting them.

The brief description of the position in the examination announcement offers some clues to the subjects which will be tested. Think about the job itself. Review the duties in your mind. Can you perform them, or are there some in which you are rusty? Fill in the blank spots in your preparation.

Many jurisdictions preview the written test in the exam announcement by including a section called "Knowledge and Abilities Required," "Scope of the Examination," or some similar heading. Here you will find out specifically what fields will be tested.

2) Review your own background

Once you learn in general what the position is all about, and what you need to know to do the work, ask yourself which subjects you already know fairly well and which need improvement. You may wonder whether to concentrate on improving your strong areas or on building some background in your fields of weakness. When the announcement has specified "some knowledge" or "considerable knowledge," or has used adjectives like "beginning principles of..." or "advanced ... methods," you can get a clue as to the number and difficulty of questions to be asked in any given field. More questions, and hence broader coverage, would be included for those subjects which are more important in the work. Now weigh your strengths and weaknesses against the job requirements and prepare accordingly.

3) Determine the level of the position

Another way to tell how intensively you should prepare is to understand the level of the job for which you are applying. Is it the entering level? In other words, is this the position in which beginners in a field of work are hired? Or is it an intermediate or advanced level? Sometimes this is indicated by such words as "Junior" or "Senior" in the class title. Other jurisdictions use Roman numerals to designate the level – Clerk I, Clerk II, for example. The word "Supervisor" sometimes appears in the title. If the level is not indicated by the title, check the description of duties. Will you be working under very close supervision, or will you have responsibility for independent decisions in this work?

4) Choose appropriate study materials

Now that you know the subjects to be examined and the relative amount of each subject to be covered, you can choose suitable study materials. For beginning level jobs, or even advanced ones, if you have a pronounced weakness in some aspect of your training, read a modern, standard textbook in that field. Be sure it is up to date and has general coverage. Such books are normally available at your library, and the librarian will be glad to help you locate one. For entry-level positions, questions of appropriate difficulty are chosen – neither highly advanced questions, nor those too simple. Such questions require careful thought but not advanced training.

If the position for which you are applying is technical or advanced, you will read more advanced, specialized material. If you are already familiar with the basic principles of your field, elementary textbooks would waste your time. Concentrate on advanced textbooks and technical periodicals. Think through the concepts and review difficult problems in your field.

These are all general sources. You can get more ideas on your own initiative, following these leads. For example, training manuals and publications of the government agency which employs workers in your field can be useful, particularly for technical and professional positions. A letter or visit to the government department involved may result in more specific study suggestions, and certainly will provide you with a more definite idea of the exact nature of the position you are seeking.

III. KINDS OF TESTS

Tests are used for purposes other than measuring knowledge and ability to perform specified duties. For some positions, it is equally important to test ability to make adjustments to new situations or to profit from training. In others, basic mental abilities not dependent on information are essential. Questions which test these things may not appear as pertinent to the duties of the position as those which test for knowledge and information. Yet they are often highly important parts of a fair examination. For very general questions, it is almost impossible to help you direct your study efforts. What we can do is to point out some of the more common of these general abilities needed in public service positions and describe some typical questions.

1) General information

Broad, general information has been found useful for predicting job success in some kinds of work. This is tested in a variety of ways, from vocabulary lists to questions about current events. Basic background in some field of work, such as sociology or economics, may be sampled in a group of questions. Often these are principles which have become familiar to most persons through exposure rather than through formal training. It is difficult to advise you how to study for these questions; being alert to the world around you is our best suggestion.

2) Verbal ability

An example of an ability needed in many positions is verbal or language ability. Verbal ability is, in brief, the ability to use and understand words. Vocabulary and grammar tests are typical measures of this ability. Reading comprehension or paragraph interpretation questions are common in many kinds of civil service tests. You are given a paragraph of written material and asked to find its central meaning.

3) Numerical ability

Number skills can be tested by the familiar arithmetic problem, by checking paired lists of numbers to see which are alike and which are different, or by interpreting charts and graphs. In the latter test, a graph may be printed in the test booklet which you are asked to use as the basis for answering questions.

4) Observation

A popular test for law-enforcement positions is the observation test. A picture is shown to you for several minutes, then taken away. Questions about the picture test your ability to observe both details and larger elements.

5) Following directions

In many positions in the public service, the employee must be able to carry out written instructions dependably and accurately. You may be given a chart with several columns, each column listing a variety of information. The questions require you to carry out directions involving the information given in the chart.

6) Skills and aptitudes

Performance tests effectively measure some manual skills and aptitudes. When the skill is one in which you are trained, such as typing or shorthand, you can practice. These tests are often very much like those given in business school or high school courses. For many of the other skills and aptitudes, however, no short-time preparation can be made. Skills and abilities natural to you or that you have developed throughout your lifetime are being tested.

Many of the general questions just described provide all the data needed to answer the questions and ask you to use your reasoning ability to find the answers. Your best preparation for these tests, as well as for tests of facts and ideas, is to be at your physical and mental best. You, no doubt, have your own methods of getting into an exam-taking mood and keeping "in shape." The next section lists some ideas on this subject.

IV. KINDS OF QUESTIONS

Only rarely is the "essay" question, which you answer in narrative form, used in civil service tests. Civil service tests are usually of the short-answer type. Full instructions for answering these questions will be given to you at the examination. But in case this is your first experience with short-answer questions and separate answer sheets, here is what you need to know:

1) Multiple-choice Questions

Most popular of the short-answer questions is the "multiple choice" or "best answer" question. It can be used, for example, to test for factual knowledge, ability to solve problems or judgment in meeting situations found at work.

A multiple-choice question is normally one of three types—
- It can begin with an incomplete statement followed by several possible endings. You are to find the one ending which *best* completes the statement, although some of the others may not be entirely wrong.
- It can also be a complete statement in the form of a question which is answered by choosing one of the statements listed.

- It can be in the form of a problem – again you select the best answer.

Here is an example of a multiple-choice question with a discussion which should give you some clues as to the method for choosing the right answer:

When an employee has a complaint about his assignment, the action which will *best* help him overcome his difficulty is to
    A. discuss his difficulty with his coworkers
    B. take the problem to the head of the organization
    C. take the problem to the person who gave him the assignment
    D. say nothing to anyone about his complaint

In answering this question, you should study each of the choices to find which is best. Consider choice "A" – Certainly an employee may discuss his complaint with fellow employees, but no change or improvement can result, and the complaint remains unresolved. Choice "B" is a poor choice since the head of the organization probably does not know what assignment you have been given, and taking your problem to him is known as "going over the head" of the supervisor. The supervisor, or person who made the assignment, is the person who can clarify it or correct any injustice. Choice "C" is, therefore, correct. To say nothing, as in choice "D," is unwise. Supervisors have and interest in knowing the problems employees are facing, and the employee is seeking a solution to his problem.

2) True/False Questions

The "true/false" or "right/wrong" form of question is sometimes used. Here a complete statement is given. Your job is to decide whether the statement is right or wrong.

SAMPLE: A roaming cell-phone call to a nearby city costs less than a non-roaming call to a distant city.

This statement is wrong, or false, since roaming calls are more expensive.
This is not a complete list of all possible question forms, although most of the others are variations of these common types. You will always get complete directions for answering questions. Be sure you understand *how* to mark your answers – ask questions until you do.

V. RECORDING YOUR ANSWERS

Computer terminals are used more and more today for many different kinds of exams.
For an examination with very few applicants, you may be told to record your answers in the test booklet itself. Separate answer sheets are much more common. If this separate answer sheet is to be scored by machine – and this is often the case – it is highly important that you mark your answers correctly in order to get credit.
An electronic scoring machine is often used in civil service offices because of the speed with which papers can be scored. Machine-scored answer sheets must be marked with a pencil, which will be given to you. This pencil has a high graphite content which responds to the electronic scoring machine. As a matter of fact, stray dots may register as answers, so do not let your pencil rest on the answer sheet while you are pondering the correct answer. Also, if your pencil lead breaks or is otherwise defective, ask for another.

Since the answer sheet will be dropped in a slot in the scoring machine, be careful not to bend the corners or get the paper crumpled.

The answer sheet normally has five vertical columns of numbers, with 30 numbers to a column. These numbers correspond to the question numbers in your test booklet. After each number, going across the page are four or five pairs of dotted lines. These short dotted lines have small letters or numbers above them. The first two pairs may also have a "T" or "F" above the letters. This indicates that the first two pairs only are to be used if the questions are of the true-false type. If the questions are multiple choice, disregard the "T" and "F" and pay attention only to the small letters or numbers.

Answer your questions in the manner of the sample that follows:

32. The largest city in the United States is
    A. Washington, D.C.
    B. New York City
    C. Chicago
    D. Detroit
    E. San Francisco

1) Choose the answer you think is best. (New York City is the largest, so "B" is correct.)
2) Find the row of dotted lines numbered the same as the question you are answering. (Find row number 32)
3) Find the pair of dotted lines corresponding to the answer. (Find the pair of lines under the mark "B.")
4) Make a solid black mark between the dotted lines.

VI. BEFORE THE TEST

Common sense will help you find procedures to follow to get ready for an examination. Too many of us, however, overlook these sensible measures. Indeed, nervousness and fatigue have been found to be the most serious reasons why applicants fail to do their best on civil service tests. Here is a list of reminders:

- Begin your preparation early – Don't wait until the last minute to go scurrying around for books and materials or to find out what the position is all about.
- Prepare continuously – An hour a night for a week is better than an all-night cram session. This has been definitely established. What is more, a night a week for a month will return better dividends than crowding your study into a shorter period of time.
- Locate the place of the exam – You have been sent a notice telling you when and where to report for the examination. If the location is in a different town or otherwise unfamiliar to you, it would be well to inquire the best route and learn something about the building.
- Relax the night before the test – Allow your mind to rest. Do not study at all that night. Plan some mild recreation or diversion; then go to bed early and get a good night's sleep.
- Get up early enough to make a leisurely trip to the place for the test – This way unforeseen events, traffic snarls, unfamiliar buildings, etc. will not upset you.
- Dress comfortably – A written test is not a fashion show. You will be known by number and not by name, so wear something comfortable.

- Leave excess paraphernalia at home – Shopping bags and odd bundles will get in your way. You need bring only the items mentioned in the official notice you received; usually everything you need is provided. Do not bring reference books to the exam. They will only confuse those last minutes and be taken away from you when in the test room.
- Arrive somewhat ahead of time – If because of transportation schedules you must get there very early, bring a newspaper or magazine to take your mind off yourself while waiting.
- Locate the examination room – When you have found the proper room, you will be directed to the seat or part of the room where you will sit. Sometimes you are given a sheet of instructions to read while you are waiting. Do not fill out any forms until you are told to do so; just read them and be prepared.
- Relax and prepare to listen to the instructions
- If you have any physical problem that may keep you from doing your best, be sure to tell the test administrator. If you are sick or in poor health, you really cannot do your best on the exam. You can come back and take the test some other time.

VII. AT THE TEST

The day of the test is here and you have the test booklet in your hand. The temptation to get going is very strong. Caution! There is more to success than knowing the right answers. You must know how to identify your papers and understand variations in the type of short-answer question used in this particular examination. Follow these suggestions for maximum results from your efforts:

1) Cooperate with the monitor

The test administrator has a duty to create a situation in which you can be as much at ease as possible. He will give instructions, tell you when to begin, check to see that you are marking your answer sheet correctly, and so on. He is not there to guard you, although he will see that your competitors do not take unfair advantage. He wants to help you do your best.

2) Listen to all instructions

Don't jump the gun! Wait until you understand all directions. In most civil service tests you get more time than you need to answer the questions. So don't be in a hurry. Read each word of instructions until you clearly understand the meaning. Study the examples, listen to all announcements and follow directions. Ask questions if you do not understand what to do.

3) Identify your papers

Civil service exams are usually identified by number only. You will be assigned a number; you must not put your name on your test papers. Be sure to copy your number correctly. Since more than one exam may be given, copy your exact examination title.

4) Plan your time

Unless you are told that a test is a "speed" or "rate of work" test, speed itself is usually not important. Time enough to answer all the questions will be provided, but this does not mean that you have all day. An overall time limit has been set. Divide the total time (in minutes) by the number of questions to determine the approximate time you have for each question.

5) Do not linger over difficult questions

If you come across a difficult question, mark it with a paper clip (useful to have along) and come back to it when you have been through the booklet. One caution if you do this – be sure to skip a number on your answer sheet as well. Check often to be sure that you have not lost your place and that you are marking in the row numbered the same as the question you are answering.

6) Read the questions

Be sure you know what the question asks! Many capable people are unsuccessful because they failed to *read* the questions correctly.

7) Answer all questions

Unless you have been instructed that a penalty will be deducted for incorrect answers, it is better to guess than to omit a question.

8) Speed tests

It is often better NOT to guess on speed tests. It has been found that on timed tests people are tempted to spend the last few seconds before time is called in marking answers at random – without even reading them – in the hope of picking up a few extra points. To discourage this practice, the instructions may warn you that your score will be "corrected" for guessing. That is, a penalty will be applied. The incorrect answers will be deducted from the correct ones, or some other penalty formula will be used.

9) Review your answers

If you finish before time is called, go back to the questions you guessed or omitted to give them further thought. Review other answers if you have time.

10) Return your test materials

If you are ready to leave before others have finished or time is called, take ALL your materials to the monitor and leave quietly. Never take any test material with you. The monitor can discover whose papers are not complete, and taking a test booklet may be grounds for disqualification.

VIII. EXAMINATION TECHNIQUES

1) Read the general instructions carefully. These are usually printed on the first page of the exam booklet. As a rule, these instructions refer to the timing of the examination; the fact that you should not start work until the signal and must stop work at a signal, etc. If there are any *special* instructions, such as a choice of questions to be answered, make sure that you note this instruction carefully.

2) When you are ready to start work on the examination, that is as soon as the signal has been given, read the instructions to each question booklet, underline any key words or phrases, such as *least*, *best*, *outline*, *describe* and the like. In this way you will tend to answer as requested rather than discover on reviewing your paper that you *listed without describing*, that you selected the *worst* choice rather than the *best* choice, etc.

3) If the examination is of the objective or multiple-choice type – that is, each question will also give a series of possible answers: A, B, C or D, and you are called upon to select the best answer and write the letter next to that answer on your answer paper – it is advisable to start answering each question in turn. There may be anywhere from 50 to 100 such questions in the three or four hours allotted and you can see how much time would be taken if you read through all the questions before beginning to answer any. Furthermore, if you come across a question or group of questions which you know would be difficult to answer, it would undoubtedly affect your handling of all the other questions.

4) If the examination is of the essay type and contains but a few questions, it is a moot point as to whether you should read all the questions before starting to answer any one. Of course, if you are given a choice – say five out of seven and the like – then it is essential to read all the questions so you can eliminate the two that are most difficult. If, however, you are asked to answer all the questions, there may be danger in trying to answer the easiest one first because you may find that you will spend too much time on it. The best technique is to answer the first question, then proceed to the second, etc.

5) Time your answers. Before the exam begins, write down the time it started, then add the time allowed for the examination and write down the time it must be completed, then divide the time available somewhat as follows:
   - If 3-1/2 hours are allowed, that would be 210 minutes. If you have 80 objective-type questions, that would be an average of 2-1/2 minutes per question. Allow yourself no more than 2 minutes per question, or a total of 160 minutes, which will permit about 50 minutes to review.
   - If for the time allotment of 210 minutes there are 7 essay questions to answer, that would average about 30 minutes a question. Give yourself only 25 minutes per question so that you have about 35 minutes to review.

6) The most important instruction is to *read each question* and make sure you know what is wanted. The second most important instruction is to *time yourself properly* so that you answer every question. The third most important instruction is to *answer every question*. Guess if you have to but include something for each question. Remember that you will receive no credit for a blank and will probably receive some credit if you write something in answer to an essay question. If you guess a letter – say "B" for a multiple-choice question – you may have guessed right. If you leave a blank as an answer to a multiple-choice question, the examiners may respect your feelings but it will not add a point to your score. Some exams may penalize you for wrong answers, so in such cases *only*, you may not want to guess unless you have some basis for your answer.

7) Suggestions
   a. Objective-type questions
      1. Examine the question booklet for proper sequence of pages and questions
      2. Read all instructions carefully
      3. Skip any question which seems too difficult; return to it after all other questions have been answered
      4. Apportion your time properly; do not spend too much time on any single question or group of questions

5. Note and underline key words – *all, most, fewest, least, best, worst, same, opposite,* etc.
6. Pay particular attention to negatives
7. Note unusual option, e.g., unduly long, short, complex, different or similar in content to the body of the question
8. Observe the use of "hedging" words – *probably, may, most likely,* etc.
9. Make sure that your answer is put next to the same number as the question
10. Do not second-guess unless you have good reason to believe the second answer is definitely more correct
11. Cross out original answer if you decide another answer is more accurate; do not erase until you are ready to hand your paper in
12. Answer all questions; guess unless instructed otherwise
13. Leave time for review

b. Essay questions
1. Read each question carefully
2. Determine exactly what is wanted. Underline key words or phrases.
3. Decide on outline or paragraph answer
4. Include many different points and elements unless asked to develop any one or two points or elements
5. Show impartiality by giving pros and cons unless directed to select one side only
6. Make and write down any assumptions you find necessary to answer the questions
7. Watch your English, grammar, punctuation and choice of words
8. Time your answers; don't crowd material

8) Answering the essay question

Most essay questions can be answered by framing the specific response around several key words or ideas. Here are a few such key words or ideas:

M's: manpower, materials, methods, money, management
P's: purpose, program, policy, plan, procedure, practice, problems, pitfalls, personnel, public relations
   a. Six basic steps in handling problems:
1. Preliminary plan and background development
2. Collect information, data and facts
3. Analyze and interpret information, data and facts
4. Analyze and develop solutions as well as make recommendations
5. Prepare report and sell recommendations
6. Install recommendations and follow up effectiveness

   b. Pitfalls to avoid
1. *Taking things for granted* – A statement of the situation does not necessarily imply that each of the elements is necessarily true; for example, a complaint may be invalid and biased so that all that can be taken for granted is that a complaint has been registered

2. *Considering only one side of a situation* – Wherever possible, indicate several alternatives and then point out the reasons you selected the best one

3. *Failing to indicate follow up* – Whenever your answer indicates action on your part, make certain that you will take proper follow-up action to see how successful your recommendations, procedures or actions turn out to be

4. *Taking too long in answering any single question* – Remember to time your answers properly

IX. AFTER THE TEST

Scoring procedures differ in detail among civil service jurisdictions although the general principles are the same. Whether the papers are hand-scored or graded by machine we have described, they are nearly always graded by number. That is, the person who marks the paper knows only the number – never the name – of the applicant. Not until all the papers have been graded will they be matched with names. If other tests, such as training and experience or oral interview ratings have been given, scores will be combined. Different parts of the examination usually have different weights. For example, the written test might count 60 percent of the final grade, and a rating of training and experience 40 percent. In many jurisdictions, veterans will have a certain number of points added to their grades.

After the final grade has been determined, the names are placed in grade order and an eligible list is established. There are various methods for resolving ties between those who get the same final grade – probably the most common is to place first the name of the person whose application was received first. Job offers are made from the eligible list in the order the names appear on it. You will be notified of your grade and your rank as soon as all these computations have been made. This will be done as rapidly as possible.

People who are found to meet the requirements in the announcement are called "eligibles." Their names are put on a list of eligible candidates. An eligible's chances of getting a job depend on how high he stands on this list and how fast agencies are filling jobs from the list.

When a job is to be filled from a list of eligibles, the agency asks for the names of people on the list of eligibles for that job. When the civil service commission receives this request, it sends to the agency the names of the three people highest on this list. Or, if the job to be filled has specialized requirements, the office sends the agency the names of the top three persons who meet these requirements from the general list.

The appointing officer makes a choice from among the three people whose names were sent to him. If the selected person accepts the appointment, the names of the others are put back on the list to be considered for future openings.

That is the rule in hiring from all kinds of eligible lists, whether they are for typist, carpenter, chemist, or something else. For every vacancy, the appointing officer has his choice of any one of the top three eligibles on the list. This explains why the person whose name is on top of the list sometimes does not get an appointment when some of the persons lower on the list do. If the appointing officer chooses the second or third eligible, the No. 1 eligible does not get a job at once, but stays on the list until he is appointed or the list is terminated.

X. HOW TO PASS THE INTERVIEW TEST

The examination for which you applied requires an oral interview test. You have already taken the written test and you are now being called for the interview test – the final part of the formal examination.

You may think that it is not possible to prepare for an interview test and that there are no procedures to follow during an interview. Our purpose is to point out some things you can do in advance that will help you and some good rules to follow and pitfalls to avoid while you are being interviewed.

What is an interview supposed to test?

The written examination is designed to test the technical knowledge and competence of the candidate; the oral is designed to evaluate intangible qualities, not readily measured otherwise, and to establish a list showing the relative fitness of each candidate – as measured against his competitors – for the position sought. Scoring is not on the basis of "right" and "wrong," but on a sliding scale of values ranging from "not passable" to "outstanding." As a matter of fact, it is possible to achieve a relatively low score without a single "incorrect" answer because of evident weakness in the qualities being measured.

Occasionally, an examination may consist entirely of an oral test – either an individual or a group oral. In such cases, information is sought concerning the technical knowledges and abilities of the candidate, since there has been no written examination for this purpose. More commonly, however, an oral test is used to supplement a written examination.

Who conducts interviews?

The composition of oral boards varies among different jurisdictions. In nearly all, a representative of the personnel department serves as chairman. One of the members of the board may be a representative of the department in which the candidate would work. In some cases, "outside experts" are used, and, frequently, a businessman or some other representative of the general public is asked to serve. Labor and management or other special groups may be represented. The aim is to secure the services of experts in the appropriate field.

However the board is composed, it is a good idea (and not at all improper or unethical) to ascertain in advance of the interview who the members are and what groups they represent. When you are introduced to them, you will have some idea of their backgrounds and interests, and at least you will not stutter and stammer over their names.

What should be done before the interview?

While knowledge about the board members is useful and takes some of the surprise element out of the interview, there is other preparation which is more substantive. It *is* possible to prepare for an oral interview – in several ways:

1) Keep a copy of your application and review it carefully before the interview

This may be the only document before the oral board, and the starting point of the interview. Know what education and experience you have listed there, and the sequence and dates of all of it. Sometimes the board will ask you to review the highlights of your experience for them; you should not have to hem and haw doing it.

2) Study the class specification and the examination announcement

Usually, the oral board has one or both of these to guide them. The qualities, characteristics or knowledges required by the position sought are stated in these documents. They offer valuable clues as to the nature of the oral interview. For example, if the job involves supervisory responsibilities, the announcement will usually indicate that knowledge of modern supervisory methods and the qualifications of the candidate as a supervisor will be tested. If so, you can expect such questions, frequently in the form of a hypothetical situation which you are expected to solve. NEVER go into an oral without knowledge of the duties and responsibilities of the job you seek.

3) Think through each qualification required

Try to visualize the kind of questions you would ask if you were a board member. How well could you answer them? Try especially to appraise your own knowledge and background in each area, *measured against the job sought*, and identify any areas in which you are weak. Be critical and realistic – do not flatter yourself.

4) Do some general reading in areas in which you feel you may be weak

For example, if the job involves supervision and your past experience has NOT, some general reading in supervisory methods and practices, particularly in the field of human relations, might be useful. Do NOT study agency procedures or detailed manuals. The oral board will be testing your understanding and capacity, not your memory.

5) Get a good night's sleep and watch your general health and mental attitude

You will want a clear head at the interview. Take care of a cold or any other minor ailment, and of course, no hangovers.

What should be done on the day of the interview?

Now comes the day of the interview itself. Give yourself plenty of time to get there. Plan to arrive somewhat ahead of the scheduled time, particularly if your appointment is in the fore part of the day. If a previous candidate fails to appear, the board might be ready for you a bit early. By early afternoon an oral board is almost invariably behind schedule if there are many candidates, and you may have to wait. Take along a book or magazine to read, or your application to review, but leave any extraneous material in the waiting room when you go in for your interview. In any event, relax and compose yourself.

The matter of dress is important. The board is forming impressions about you – from your experience, your manners, your attitude, and your appearance. Give your personal appearance careful attention. Dress your best, but not your flashiest. Choose conservative, appropriate clothing, and be sure it is immaculate. This is a business interview, and your appearance should indicate that you regard it as such. Besides, being well groomed and properly dressed will help boost your confidence.

Sooner or later, someone will call your name and escort you into the interview room. *This is it.* From here on you are on your own. It is too late for any more preparation. But remember, you asked for this opportunity to prove your fitness, and you are here because your request was granted.

What happens when you go in?

The usual sequence of events will be as follows: The clerk (who is often the board stenographer) will introduce you to the chairman of the oral board, who will introduce you to the other members of the board. Acknowledge the introductions before you sit down. Do not be surprised if you find a microphone facing you or a stenotypist sitting by. Oral interviews are usually recorded in the event of an appeal or other review.

Usually the chairman of the board will open the interview by reviewing the highlights of your education and work experience from your application – primarily for the benefit of the other members of the board, as well as to get the material into the record. Do not interrupt or comment unless there is an error or significant misinterpretation; if that is the case, do not hesitate. But do not quibble about insignificant matters. Also, he will usually ask you some question about your education, experience or your present job – partly to get you to start talking and to establish the interviewing "rapport." He may start the actual questioning, or turn it over to one of the other members. Frequently, each member undertakes the questioning on a particular area, one in which he is perhaps most competent, so you can expect each member to participate in the examination. Because time is limited, you may also expect some rather abrupt switches in the direction the questioning takes, so do not be upset by it. Normally, a board member will not pursue a single line of questioning unless he discovers a particular strength or weakness.

After each member has participated, the chairman will usually ask whether any member has any further questions, then will ask you if you have anything you wish to add. Unless you are expecting this question, it may floor you. Worse, it may start you off on an extended, extemporaneous speech. The board is not usually seeking more information. The question is principally to offer you a last opportunity to present further qualifications or to indicate that you have nothing to add. So, if you feel that a significant qualification or characteristic has been overlooked, it is proper to point it out in a sentence or so. Do not compliment the board on the thoroughness of their examination – they have been sketchy, and you know it. If you wish, merely say, "No thank you, I have nothing further to add." This is a point where you can "talk yourself out" of a good impression or fail to present an important bit of information. Remember, *you close the interview yourself.*

The chairman will then say, "That is all, Mr. _____, thank you." Do not be startled; the interview is over, and quicker than you think. Thank him, gather your belongings and take your leave. Save your sigh of relief for the other side of the door.

How to put your best foot forward

Throughout this entire process, you may feel that the board individually and collectively is trying to pierce your defenses, seek out your hidden weaknesses and embarrass and confuse you. Actually, this is not true. They are obliged to make an appraisal of your qualifications for the job you are seeking, and they want to see you in your best light. Remember, they must interview all candidates and a non-cooperative candidate may become a failure in spite of their best efforts to bring out his qualifications. Here are 15 suggestions that will help you:

1) Be natural – Keep your attitude confident, not cocky

If you are not confident that you can do the job, do not expect the board to be. Do not apologize for your weaknesses, try to bring out your strong points. The board is interested in a positive, not negative, presentation. Cockiness will antagonize any board member and make him wonder if you are covering up a weakness by a false show of strength.

2) Get comfortable, but don't lounge or sprawl

Sit erectly but not stiffly. A careless posture may lead the board to conclude that you are careless in other things, or at least that you are not impressed by the importance of the occasion. Either conclusion is natural, even if incorrect. Do not fuss with your clothing, a pencil or an ashtray. Your hands may occasionally be useful to emphasize a point; do not let them become a point of distraction.

3) Do not wisecrack or make small talk

This is a serious situation, and your attitude should show that you consider it as such. Further, the time of the board is limited – they do not want to waste it, and neither should you.

4) Do not exaggerate your experience or abilities

In the first place, from information in the application or other interviews and sources, the board may know more about you than you think. Secondly, you probably will not get away with it. An experienced board is rather adept at spotting such a situation, so do not take the chance.

5) If you know a board member, do not make a point of it, yet do not hide it

Certainly you are not fooling him, and probably not the other members of the board. Do not try to take advantage of your acquaintanceship – it will probably do you little good.

6) Do not dominate the interview

Let the board do that. They will give you the clues – do not assume that you have to do all the talking. Realize that the board has a number of questions to ask you, and do not try to take up all the interview time by showing off your extensive knowledge of the answer to the first one.

7) Be attentive

You only have 20 minutes or so, and you should keep your attention at its sharpest throughout. When a member is addressing a problem or question to you, give him your undivided attention. Address your reply principally to him, but do not exclude the other board members.

8) Do not interrupt

A board member may be stating a problem for you to analyze. He will ask you a question when the time comes. Let him state the problem, and wait for the question.

9) Make sure you understand the question

Do not try to answer until you are sure what the question is. If it is not clear, restate it in your own words or ask the board member to clarify it for you. However, do not haggle about minor elements.

10) Reply promptly but not hastily

A common entry on oral board rating sheets is "candidate responded readily," or "candidate hesitated in replies." Respond as promptly and quickly as you can, but do not jump to a hasty, ill-considered answer.

11) Do not be peremptory in your answers

A brief answer is proper – but do not fire your answer back. That is a losing game from your point of view. The board member can probably ask questions much faster than you can answer them.

12) Do not try to create the answer you think the board member wants

He is interested in what kind of mind you have and how it works – not in playing games. Furthermore, he can usually spot this practice and will actually grade you down on it.

13) Do not switch sides in your reply merely to agree with a board member

Frequently, a member will take a contrary position merely to draw you out and to see if you are willing and able to defend your point of view. Do not start a debate, yet do not surrender a good position. If a position is worth taking, it is worth defending.

14) Do not be afraid to admit an error in judgment if you are shown to be wrong

The board knows that you are forced to reply without any opportunity for careful consideration. Your answer may be demonstrably wrong. If so, admit it and get on with the interview.

15) Do not dwell at length on your present job

The opening question may relate to your present assignment. Answer the question but do not go into an extended discussion. You are being examined for a *new* job, not your present one. As a matter of fact, try to phrase ALL your answers in terms of the job for which you are being examined.

Basis of Rating

Probably you will forget most of these "do's" and "don'ts" when you walk into the oral interview room. Even remembering them all will not ensure you a passing grade. Perhaps you did not have the qualifications in the first place. But remembering them will help you to put your best foot forward, without treading on the toes of the board members.

Rumor and popular opinion to the contrary notwithstanding, an oral board wants you to make the best appearance possible. They know you are under pressure – but they also want to see how you respond to it as a guide to what your reaction would be under the pressures of the job you seek. They will be influenced by the degree of poise you display, the personal traits you show and the manner in which you respond.

ABOUT THIS BOOK

This book contains tests divided into Examination Sections. Go through each test, answering every question in the margin. We have also attached a sample answer sheet at the back of the book that can be removed and used. At the end of each test look at the answer key and check your answers. On the ones you got wrong, look at the right answer choice and learn. Do not fill in the answers first. Do not memorize the questions and answers, but understand the answer and principles involved. On your test, the questions will likely be different from the samples. Questions are changed and new ones added. If you understand these past questions you should have success with any changes that arise. Tests may consist of several types of questions. We have additional books on each subject should more study be advisable or necessary for you. Finally, the more you study, the better prepared you will be. This book is intended to be the last thing you study before you walk into the examination room. Prior study of relevant texts is also recommended. NLC publishes some of these in our Fundamental Series. Knowledge and good sense are important factors in passing your exam. Good luck also helps. So now study this Passbook, absorb the material contained within and take that knowledge into the examination. Then do your best to pass that exam.

———

EXAMINATION SECTION

EXAMINATION SECTION
TEST 1

DIRECTIONS: Each question or incomplete statement is followed by several suggested answers or completions. Select the one that BEST answers the question or completes the statement. *PRINT THE LETTER OF THE CORRECT ANSWER IN THE SPACE AT THE RIGHT.*

1. Assume that, as a probation officer, you are assigned a pre-sentence investigation. In preparation for the initial interview with the defendant, you should FIRST   1._____

   A. send through a call sheet to the Department of Correction requesting that the defendant be produced for an interview
   B. secure a copy of the fingerprint report from the Police Department
   C. secure a copy of the indictment or criminal information from the District Attorney
   D. collect all available information about the defendant from the court docket, District Attorney file, police records, and report of offense

2. According to accepted practice, the probation officer explains the conditions of probation and the functions of the Department of Probation to the adult probationer during the initial interview.   2._____
   Of the following, the CHIEF advantage of using this approach is that it

   A. serves as a convenient starting point in a new relationship
   B. places the new probationer on guard to avoid possible violations of probation
   C. eliminates the need to give the probationer written explanatory material
   D. assists in gaining the cooperation of the new probationer to help himself

3. Although an investigating probation officer may not be able to control the conditions under which he conducts an interview with a defendant or a collateral source of information, it is sometimes possible to select the site of the interview. Assume that a defendant is at liberty and it is necessary to secure information from him and from members of his family.   3._____
   It would be PREFERABLE to

   A. set up an appointment for the defendant to see you at your office, scheduling a home visit later when the defendant is not at home
   B. set up a home visit where all members of the family, including the defendant, can be interviewed at once
   C. make a surprise home visit so the family and the defendant cannot *set the stage* for you in order to make a good impression
   D. call the defendant and the appropriate relatives into the office for a consecutive series of interviews, both individually and collectively

4. Assume that you are conducting an initial interview at a young probationer's home early in the evening. The mother of your client invites you to stay for dinner.   4._____
   Of the following, your MOST appropriate response would be to

   A. *accept,* since it will give you an opportunity to become better acquainted with the probationer's family
   B. *decline,* explaining that you are not hungry, but tell the family you will be glad to stay for coffee
   C. *accept,* since refusal of the invitation might be construed as rejection
   D. *decline,* since acceptance of the invitation might interfere with performance of your professional role

5. Assume that you are supervising an adult probationer convicted of involuntary man-
slaughter, who is required to secure employment as a condition of probation. The probationer brings you an application given to him by a prospective employer, and asks you
how much information he should divulge on the application with regard to his arrest, con-
viction, and probation.
As his supervising probation officer, you should instruct the probationer to

   A. leave that part of the application blank
   B. place an X in the arrest and convictions section, but give no other details
   C. include all the details, but explain that he has never been in trouble for stealing,
      since this is probably the employer's main concern
   D. fill out the application honestly and refer the employer to you if he has any further
      questions

6. Assume that a probation officer is interviewing a client who seems to be unable to hold a
job for any length of time and has quit his most recent job after only two weeks.
In order to encourage the client to talk about this situation, of the following, it would be
MOST appropriate for the probation officer to say,

   A. Did you quit that job because you weren't getting enough money?
   B. Tell me some of the reasons why you quit that job.
   C. Did your wife say anything when you quit that job?
   D. Well, I guess you will have to get busy and find another job.

7. A probation officer is interviewing a young male client who seems to be having difficulty
describing how he got into his current life situation. When the probation officer asks him
to tell his story, the client says,
I am not sure if I can explain how I got into this mess. Which of the following would be
the probation officer's MOST appropriate response?

   A. Well, it may not be so important.
   B. Well, then, perhaps we can go on to something else.
   C. Well, we have very limited time.
   D. Well, tell it your own way and perhaps I can help you as you go along.

8. Assume that you are interviewing a new probationer for the first time. Initially, his answers
to your routine questions are purposefully and continuously evasive and hostile.
In questioning this probationer further, the MOST appropriate of the following courses
of action for you to take would be to

   A. refrain from responding to this provocative or *testing* behavior
   B. suggest that the interview be postponed until the probationer is ready to answer
      your questions in a forthright manner
   C. insist that the probationer tell you why he is being uncooperative
   D. warn the probationer that you will recommend a revocation of probation if he con-
      tinues being evasive

9. To what extent should note-taking GENERALLY be used during an initial interview with a
new probationer?

   A. All information the offender offers should be recorded.
   B. Essential confidential information only should be recorded.
   C. Notes should be taken on routine data only, and the remainder recorded later.
   D. Only information likely to be forgotten should be recorded.

10. Assume that a new probationer objects to certain rules and regulations concerning his conditions of probation.
    Of the following, the MOST effective way to handle these objections initially, while maintaining the probationer's active willing cooperation, is to

    A. explain that all probationers must comply with certain conditions and that the probation officer cannot modify or change them
    B. remind him that his probation might be revoked if he does not comply
    C. point out that compliance with probation conditions often results in early release from probation
    D. explore and evaluate his objections, while explaining the reasons for the rules and regulations

10.____

11. Assume that you are a probation officer interviewing a new probationer who is considerably older than you. Early in the interview, the probationer starts to reminisce about the *good old days.*
    You should consider this reminiscing on the part of the probationer to be

    A. *beneficial,* because it may have the effect of reducing the existing age difference, which could be a barrier to successful interviewing
    B. *harmful,* because the probationer has already been convicted and should stick to the subject of the discussion as you direct
    C. *beneficial,* because it may have the effect of eliminating guilt feelings the probationer might have about his crime
    D. *harmful,* because it may have a negative and depressing psychological effect on both you and the probationer

11.____

12. With regard to the chances of establishing a good relationship in an interview situation between a client and a probation officer of the same or opposite sex, studies have GENERALLY shown that

    A. there are fewer barriers between a male client and a female probation officer than between a female client and a male probation officer
    B. there are fewer barriers between a male client and a female probation officer than between a male client and a male probation officer
    C. the sex of the parties has no bearing on the information obtained or topics discussed
    D. there may be barriers due to the difference in sex, but they can usually be overcome by a skillful interviewer

12.____

13. As an investigating probation officer, you are interviewing the mother of a juvenile offender in the family's small apartment. The mother is confused and upset as a result of her son's difficulties and she has not been able to answer several essential questions satisfactorily. Your BEST course of action in this situation is to

    A. ask these questions again at the next interview when the mother should hopefully be less upset
    B. repeat these questions patiently until the necessary information is brought to light
    C. firmly impress upon the mother that you cannot terminate the interview until she has answered the questions
    D. refer the mother to a family agency where she can receive counseling for her problems about her son

13.____

14. Assume that you are a probation officer interviewing an adult defendant who is due for   14.___
    sentencing. Since the defendant was unable to post bail, the interview takes place in the
    defendant's cell, and the surroundings are physically uncomfortable.
    In order to put the defendant at ease and secure as much information as possible from
    him, it would be MOST helpful for you to

    A. talk in an authoritative voice to impress the defendant with the seriousness of his
        situation
    B. try to disregard the surroundings and appear relaxed, while focusing on the inter-
        view
    C. act in a businesslike manner and handle the interview as though you were in your
        office
    D. ask a fellow inmate to witness the interview, to make the defendant feel more com-
        fortable

15. Which one of the following types of questions would generally be considered INEFFEC-   15.___
    TIVE during an interview with a defendant?

    A. Questions which require a *yes* or *no* answer
    B. Open-ended questions which require some explanation
    C. Questions that might be difficult for the defendant to answer
    D. Questions which have emotional connotations

16. It is generally agreed that, when verifying information given to you by a defendant, it is   16.___
    best to have the defendant's concurrence before checking with certain sources, such as
    a previous employer.
    If a defendant disagrees with your decision after you have explained your reason for
    considering a contact essential for your pre-sentence report, it would generally be
    MOST appropriate for you to

    A. contact the source despite the defendant's objection
    B. respect the defendant's wishes and not make the disputed contact
    C. ask the defendant to get the information for you in writing
    D. postpone the contact and try to convince the defendant to agree at a later date

17. Assume that, during the course of your pre-sentence investigation of a defendant, you   17.___
    find that the complainant, who was the defendant's victim, is guilty of contributing to the
    offense for which the defendant was convicted.
    In preparing your pre-sentence report relative to this finding, of the following, the BEST
    practice would be to

    A. include all significant information about the complainant's involvement
    B. omit any reference to the complainant's involvement
    C. make only a brief reference to the complainant's involvement
    D. give your interpretation of the complainant's motivation

18. It is generally considered appropriate for the probation officer to use non-directive, open   18.___
    questions during the early part of the interview with the probationer MAINLY because
    such questions

    A. allow the probationer to choose his own approach to the content of the question
    B. impose heavier demands on the probationer to tell his story fully
    C. help the probationer to select and organize his responses
    D. encourage responses that are factual and brief

19. In order to conduct a successful interview with a client, the probation officer must decide to what degree the interview should be structured and controlled.
Of the following, the MOST likely effect of a highly structured interview is to

    A. provoke anxiety and hostility in the client
    B. lessen the client's confidence and cooperativeness
    C. reduce anxiety and increase the client's confidence
    D. violate the client's integrity and right of self-determination

19.____

20. The QUICKEST and MOST informative of the following methods of determining how a juvenile defendant relates to other members of his immediate family is to

    A. interview the defendant
    B. interview members of the defendant's immediate family
    C. have a staff psychologist administer projective tests to the defendant
    D. construct a sociogram of the immediate family

20.____

21. Assume that, during an interview with a young male client, a probation officer wants to change the subject under discussion and go back to another, more important topic which the client brought up earlier in the interview.
In directing the discussion back to the earlier subject, it would be MOST advisable for the probation officer to

    A. comment on it without mentioning that the client was talking about the subject before, mainly because the client may realize that he was avoiding this topic and refuse to go back to it
    B. use the previous comments and, if possible, even the client's own words about the more important subject, mainly because this suggests that the probationer has shared responsibility for going back to it
    C. summarize in his own words the material just discussed by the client, mainly because this will help him to become aware that he has exhausted it and should go back to the other subject
    D. inform the client that he cannot avoid talking about the topic discussed earlier in the interview, mainly because this will make him aware of the importance of this subject

21.____

22. A common error made by inexperienced probation officers in their early interviews is to talk too much, and give the interviewee too little opportunity to talk.
In order to listen effectively, the probation officer should do all of the following with the EXCEPTION of

    A. following what is being said overtly
    B. following the latent overtones of what is being said
    C. assuming that he knows what is going to be said
    D. acting relaxed but alert and attentive to what is said

22.____

23. Assume that a probation officer has received reports from a young female probationer's employer that she is not getting along with her fellow workers. During the weekly interview, the probation officer attempts to focus on this problem, but the probationer persistently digresses from the subject of her job.
In this situation, of the following, it would be MOST appropriate for the probation officer to say

    A. That's interesting, and perhaps we can come back to it later. However, it may be more helpful if we could talk about the way you get along on your job.
    B. Now, let's not change the subject. Your boss tells me you're not getting along with the people at work and you will be in trouble if you get yourself fired.
    C. You're changing the subject because you don't want to talk about your job. That's the important thing right now, and we can't waste time discussing anything else.
    D. You know, I have six more interviews today, and I only have time to discuss things that might affect your probation. So let's get back to talking about the trouble on your job.

23.___

24. In considering the use of religion to assist the probationer, the probation officer should

    A. include church attendance as a prerequisite in the treatment plan
    B. not try to develop a religious connection through the use of his legal authority
    C. require the probationer to attend church for a trial period
    D. never use religion as a community resource or as a subject of discussion with the probationer

24.___

25. Assume that a probation officer has learned that a young male probationer under his supervision is not following the instructions of the court about his recreational activities, and has been associating with his former companions at a pool hall which has a bad reputation.
At the next interview, of the following actions, it would be MOST advisable for the probation officer to

    A. tell the probationer that he has violated probation and warn him that he will be penalized if he does not obey the court
    B. tell the probationer that he is aware of his activities, and that he plans to watch him more closely in the future
    C. try to get the probationer to discuss his feelings about his companions, his interests, and his recreational activities
    D. avoid discussing the probationer's leisure time activities unless he brings up the subject himself

25.___

KEY (CORRECT ANSWERS)

1.	D		11.	A
2.	A		12.	D
3.	A		13.	B
4.	D		14.	B
5.	D		15.	A
6.	B		16.	A
7.	D		17.	A
8.	A		18.	A
9.	C		19.	C
10.	D		20.	C

21.	B
22.	C
23.	A
24.	B
25.	C

————

TEST 2

DIRECTIONS: Each question or incomplete statement is followed by several suggested answers or completions. Select the one that BEST answers the question or completes the statement. *PRINT THE LETTER OF THE CORRECT ANSWER IN THE SPACE AT THE RIGHT.*

1. Assume that a probation officer is interviewing a female juvenile offender who is being sent to a residential treatment center by order of the court. During the interview, she tells the probation officer that she will do her best to escape soon after she arrives at the center. The BEST course of action for the probation officer to take would be to

    A. advise the girl that she will be committed to a state training school if she tries to escape
    B. accept the girl's statement as part of her total behavior, but tell her that you will share this information with the treatment center
    C. pay no attention to the girl's statement and allow the treatment center to handle her attempts to escape
    D. ignore the girl's statement since escaping from the treatment center will be much more difficult than she thinks

1.____

2. The one of the following which is generally considered to be the MOST important factor in the selection of probation as an alternative to institutionalization is the offender's

    A. age   B. motivation for adjustment
    C. family relationships   D. history of arrests

2.____

3. The suggestion has been made that probation agencies, like many private casework agencies, should adopt the practice of charging a modest fee for probation service. Of the following, the MOST valid reason why this practice could serve a useful purpose is that

    A. probationers would have additional pressure to earn a living by legitimate means
    B. fee payment would give the probationer an opportunity to meet his financial responsibilities
    C. fees collected from probationers would make a substantial contribution to public funds
    D. payment of a modest fee would help the probationer maintain his self-respect and do his best to benefit from probation

3.____

4. Which of the following is the MOST important reason why the rules and regulations applying to probation facilitate rehabilitation of the probationer?
The

    A. probationer can derive emotional security from knowing, *I can go so far, but no further*
    B. probation officer can base his authority on statutes established by his department
    C. probationer can be penalized for infractions without being referred back to court
    D. probation officer can refer to a clear statement of the functions and aims of probation

4.____

5. Experts generally believe that rules and regulations applying to probationers are MOST useful when they are

5.____

A. adapted uniformly to all probationers
B. adapted to the needs of the given individual and to the conditions
C. expressed in negative rather than positive terms
D. phrased in positive terms even when they are not always rigidly enforced

6. Assume that during the course of a pre-sentence investigation you receive a telephone call from the brother of a defendant, asking you to visit him at his place of business, a women's coat factory, with regard to his brother's case. During the visit, the defendant's brother offers to give you a *good price* on a new coat for your wife.
Of the following responses, it would be MOST appropriate for the probation officer to   6._____

A. *refuse,* because your pre-sentence report on the defendant may be unfavorable
B. *accept,* because the coat is not offered as an outright gift
C. *refuse,* since the brother's offer may be construed as an attempt to influence the nature of the pre-sentence report
D. *accept,* since you will be able to make a note of this offer in the case record, which is submitted to the court

7. In the city, probation work is divided into three phases or points in the legal process, which include   7._____

A. investigation, supervision, and correction
B. intake, supervision, and reporting
C. supervision, correction, and intake
D. intake, investigation, and supervision

8. Of the following, an investigating probation officer assigned to conduct a pre-sentence investigation for the court is MAINLY responsible for   8._____

A. developing a full story of the offense and the defendant's participation so that the judge can impose appropriate punishment
B. convincing the defendant that he has done wrong and is about to receive just punishment for his crime
C. providing the court with an account of the defendant's participation in the crime, motivation, and previous life style
D. recommending to the court what he believes to be an appropriate disposition of the case

9. Assume that a probation officer has determined that one of his probationers, who is not psychotic, requires psychiatric treatment.
Of the following, the MOST appropriate action for the probation officer to take is to   9._____

A. refer the probationer to a psychiatric treatment center and order him to make an appointment
B. interpret to the probationer his need for psychiatric therapy in an effort to have him take the initiative in entering treatment
C. make an appointment at a psychiatric treatment center for the probationer and accompany him to the first visit
D. stipulate to the probationer that his acceptance of psychiatric treatment will be a condition of probation

10. Assume that, during the course of a pre-sentence investigation, you, as a probation officer, make a pre-arranged visit to an offender's residence to obtain a clear picture of the way he lives. In addition to the offender, family members are also present. Statements made by family members in response to your questions should GENERALLY be considered to be LACKING in

    A. vindictiveness   B. protectiveness
    C. bias   D. objectivity

10.____

11. Suppose you are interviewing a male defendant for the purpose of preparing a pre-sentence investigation report. Based on what he has told you so far, you believe that his chances for probation are good. A little later in the interview, the defendant expresses concern for his wife's ability to support herself and their three children if he is sentenced to a jail term.
Of the following, your BEST initial response to the defendant's concern would be as follows:

    A. Why didn't you consider this possibility before you committed the offense?
    B. You're right. It won't be easy to manage, but help may be available to her if she is in need.
    C. Don't worry. Everything will be all right.
    D. Based on what you've told me, your chances for probation are good.

11.____

12. Authorities in the field of probation generally emphasize the concept that it is essential for the probation officer to have an accepting, nonjudgmental attitude in order to maintain a positive and helpful relationship with his clients.
Of the following, the MOST valid description of this concept is that the probation officer

    A. is concerned with understanding, rather than praising or blaming the client
    B. agrees with the client's point of view and his concept of reality
    C. resists making generalizations about the client
    D. communicates confidence in the client's ability to direct his own life

12.____

13. Assume that, during a conference with his supervisor, a newly appointed probation officer expresses concern because he feels antagonistic and anxious in the presence of one of his clients, and these feelings tend to cause problems during the interview. The supervisor suggests that this may be due to counter-transference, a psychological concept which means that negative feelings are activated because the probation officer

    A. overidentifies with the client and his difficulties
    B. associates the client with some significant person in his own past
    C. has a preconceived judgment about the client's ethnic group
    D. believes that the client is hostile and angry with him

13.____

14. The interviewing technique called *clarification* would be PROPERLY used by a probation officer in counseling a probationer who

    A. has trouble verbalizing his feelings
    B. requires reassurance and encouragement
    C. is confused about the significance of his thoughts
    D. needs discipline and firm treatment

14.____

15. According to accepted practice, in preparing a pre-sentence investigation report it is con- 15._____
sidered advisable for the probation officer to interview the complainant, MAINLY because
the complainant is likely to

    A. give the most objective account of the crime
    B. be the primary source of information about the crime
    C. have been a participant in the crime
    D. suggest the most suitable sentence for the crime

16. Assume that you have made an appointment for a 3 P.M. home visit to a female proba- 16._____
tioner with a young child, but find that you will be delayed about an hour by a backlog of
interviews in your office.
In this situation, it would be MOST advisable to

    A. telephone the probationer and ask her to see you in your office the next morning
instead
    B. visit the probationer an hour later than the scheduled appointment, without phon-
ing first
    C. telephone the probationer as soon as you know you will be delayed and tell her
that you will be about an hour late
    D. cancel your present appointment by telephone and make another appointment for
the next week

17. Assume that a probation officer is aware that a client, who is an alcoholic, has been lying 17._____
to him about participating in drinking sessions during the previous week. During the interview, it would be ADVISABLE for the probation officer to _____ the client says, mainly
because the _____.

    A. *accept;* probation officer will jeopardize his relationship with the client if he ques-
tions the client's veracity
    B. *question;* probation officer would not be able to use his authority effectively to help
the client if he accepts the lie
    C. *accept;* client will lose confidence in the probation officer if he questions the lie
    D. *question;* client may think he is ready for discharge from probation if the probation
officer accepts the lie

18. Assume that, as a probation officer, you are conducting a supervision interview with a 18._____
juvenile offender who acts cocky, and deliberately makes provoking remarks. Finally, he
says, *you people can't do a thing to me because I've been here before and I know my
rights as a juvenile.* Of the following, your BEST reaction to this attitude and behavior
would be to say:

    A. I can understand how you feel, but wouldn't you like to tell me why you seem to be
so angry?
    B. If you know what's good for you, you'll cooperate with me, because you may not get
away so easily this time.
    C. Your rights may be important to you, but the rights of society must also be pro-
tected.
    D. You're absolutely correct, but I'm getting paid to try to rehabilitate you, if at all pos-
sible.

19. Assume that an emotional topic is being discussed with a probation officer during the   19._____
    course of an interview with a defendant, and the defendant stops talking suddenly.
    A 30-second silence follows.
    In this situation, of the following, it is usually MOST important for the probation officer
    to

    A. try to understand the meaning of the silence and respond accordingly
    B. ask another question on the subject being discussed
    C. ask a question about a new subject
    D. talk about his own experiences regarding the subject under discussion

20. It is important for the probation officer to recognize and understand a client's feelings of   20._____
    ambivalence.
    The behavioral manifestation of ambivalence that appears MOST frequently in the pro-
    bation interview is

    A. timidity   B. indecision
    C. arrogance   D. hostility

21. Studies have confirmed that race and sex differences between interviewer and inter-   21._____
    viewee present inherent barriers to effective interviewing, varying in degree. The MOST
    potentially problematic of the following combinations is a _____ client interviewed by a
    _____ probation officer.

    A. black male; black female
    B. white female; white male
    C. black male; white female
    D. white female; black female

22. Assume that one of your cases is a middle-aged Puerto Rican woman whose period of   22._____
    probation is almost completed. She speaks very little English, and you have not been
    able to motivate her to attend the night school English classes which you have recom-
    mended. However, she is steadily employed as a seamstress, does not need English on
    her job or in her predominantly Spanish neighborhood, and has otherwise made a satis-
    factory adjustment within her limitations.
    Of the following, the MOST appropriate course of action for you to take to benefit this
    probationer would be to

    A. suggest to your supervisor that she be transferred to a Spanish-speaking probation
        officer
    B. recommend discharge when her period of probation is over
    C. report her to the court for failure to attend English classes
    D. offer her an early discharge from probation if she attends English classes

23. Sociotherapy, a highly effective technique especially useful for persons with limited   23._____
    expressive ability, is distinguished from psychotherapy in that sociotherapy deals
    MAINLY with

    A. changing a client's ability to cope with a situation
    B. changing a situation so that it is easier to handle
    C. restructuring the client's basic attitudes toward social institutions
    D. developing a theoretical Utopian social status the client can strive to achieve

24. During an interview with a probationer of low income and education levels, to facilitate understanding your questions should GENERALLY be formulated so as to focus on which of the following types of information?

    A. Abstract details   B. Symbolic activities
    C. Concrete situations   D. Introspective matters

24.____

25. In order for a middle-class, white probation officer to conduct a meaningful, successful interview with a lower class, black probationer, the probation officer's manner of speaking should be

    A. the same as his usual manner, but include colloquialisms such as *jive* and *rap*
    B. the same as his usual manner when talking to a layman or any other probationer
    C. different from his usual manner in that he should use simpler language
    D. different from his usual manner in that he should be more formal

25.____

KEY (CORRECT ANSWERS)

1.	B		11.	B
2.	B		12.	A
3.	D		13.	B
4.	A		14.	C
5.	B		15.	B
6.	C		16.	C
7.	D		17.	B
8.	C		18.	A
9.	B		19.	A
10.	D		20.	B

21.	C
22.	B
23.	B
24.	C
25.	B

EXAMINATION SECTION
TEST 1

DIRECTIONS: Each question or incomplete statement is followed by several suggested answers or completions. Select the one that BEST answers the question or completes the statement. *PRINT THE LETTER OF THE CORRECT ANSWER IN THE SPACE AT THE RIGHT.*

1. Assume that you are conducting an initial interview with a married couple, both much younger than yourself, who are low-income people with very little formal education. As the husband's supervising probation officer, it would be MOST appropriate for you to address them as (or by)

   A. their first names, since this is how they are accustomed to being addressed
   B. *Mr.* and *Mrs.* and their last name, since this is a sign of seriousness and sincerity
   C. the husband's last name and the wife's first name, since this is the traditional manner in this couple's social group
   D. *sir* and *madam,* to emphasize the formality of the situation

1.____

2. In addition to other identifying data, the face sheet of a pre-sentence report should contain information relative to a defendant's age and marital status. Which of the following is the MOST appropriate entry which should be included on the face sheet of a pre-sentence report?
   Age -

   A. 35, Marital status - divorced, 3/6/14
   B. 35, Born - 7/12/79, Marital status - divorced
   C. 35, Marital status - divorced, 3/6/14, expected to remarry 9/15
   D. 35, Born - 7/12/79, Marital status - divorced, 3/6/14, mental cruelty

2.____

3. Which one of the following statements BEST describes the proper scope of information about a defendant's numerous brothers and sisters which should be included in a pre-sentence report?

   A. Complete listing of names, dates of birth, occupations and residences by city and state of all brothers and sisters
   B. A listing of names, dates of birth, occupations, and residences by city and state of the brothers and sisters who might influence the defendant if placed on probation
   C. Data as stated in option A and a narrative summary on those who have had or are likely to have an influence on the defendant
   D. A narrative summary on only those brothers and sisters likely to have a positive or negative influence on the defendant if placed on probation

3.____

4. Assume that you are preparing a pre-sentence report. Two pieces of related information have come to your attention, in addition to the routine listing of arrests and convictions. The first piece of information comes from the police, who inform you that they have had strong reason to suspect your defendant of other offenses, but could never obtain enough evidence to arrest the defendant. The source of the second piece of information is a neighbor, who tells you, in confidence, that he witnessed the defendant cheat and steal from merchants, and get into fights, but no actual arrests were made. These offenses occurred at a different time from the offenses referred to by the police. Which of

4.____

these additional pieces of information, if any, should be included in your pre-sentence report?

    A. The first *only*   B. The second *only*
    C. Both   D. Neither

5. Assume that you are gathering data for a pre-sentence report on a 21-year-old defen-   5.____
dant. You have learned as a result of a visit to his high school that the defendant had severe serious emotional problems during the last half of his senior year.
The MOST appropriate of the following sections of your report in which to include this information is the section on

    A. psychological health   B. physical health
    C. education   D. medical history

6. A psychiatrist's diagnosis of a defendant's mental health should be presented in a pre-   6.____
sentence investigation report in the form of a(n)

    A. paraphrase of the psychiatrist's statements, using layman's terminology
    B. interpretation by the probation officer of the psychiatrist's evaluation
    C. direct quotation of the psychiatrist's diagnosis
    D. statement by the probation officer appraising the defendant's mental health

7. Which one of the following is NOT a purpose of the pre-sentence investigation report?   7.____
To

    A. aid the court in sentencing the defendant
    B. determine the guilt or innocence of the defendant
    C. assist eventually in planning for release of the defendant
    D. provide data for research in the field of criminal justice

8. Sexual conduct, may be a difficult and often embarrassing subject to investigate and   8.____
report on.
Which one of the following statements BEST describes the scope of information which should be included in a pre-sentence report concerning a sexual offense?

    A. Terms such as *rape* or *sexual perversion* should be used in lieu of more explicit details, as these are universally understood and usually suffice.
    B. Sexual acts should be described explicitly to give a clear, objective account of what transpired, including both parties' versions.
    C. The defendant's version should be included, but the victim's testimony ommitted, since it is usually too embarrassing to elicit.
    D. The information should be limited to that contained in the charges or indictment, as the participants' versions are usually subjective and misleading.

9. In preparing a pre-sentence report, of the following, a probation officer should place PRI-   9.____
MARY emphasis on

    A. major events in the life of the offender from birth
    B. the meaning the offender has derived from his life experiences
    C. the psychological profile of the offender
    D. a chronological history of all circumstances leading to the offender's arrest and conviction

10. The PRIMARY purpose of a pre-sentence investigation report by a probation officer is to   10.____

    A. serve as a future plan of treatment for the offender
    B. assist the court in making an appropriate disposition of a case
    C. protect society from the offender
    D. protect the offender's legal rights

11. In making a recommendation to the court on probation for an adult offender, of the follow-   11.____
ing, the criterion that should generally be given the LEAST consideration is the

    A. protection of the community
    B. type of offense committed
    C. prospect of reforming the offender
    D. background of the offender

12. A pre-sentence investigation report usually includes a description of the offense commit-   12.____
ted by the defendant.
Which one of the following sources would usually be considered LEAST reliable for
this section of the report?

    A. The defendant   B. Police records
    C. The complainant   D. Eyewitnesses

13. Which one of the following types of information would MOST likely be found on a face   13.____
sheet?

    A. Medical and mental examination reports
    B. Identifying data about the offender
    C. A synthesis of the case record
    D. Identifying data about the complainant

14. Assume that a probation officer has included a verbatim transcription of a probationer's   14.____
indictment in his investigation report.
This practice is GENERALLY considered

    A. *desirable,* mainly because inclusion of the indictment completes the picture of the
probationer's situation
    B. *undesirable,* mainly because a transcript of the indictment is available to the court
if needed
    C. *desirable,* mainly because inclusion of the document itself is the best guarantee of
objectivity
    D. *undesirable,* mainly because the court already has knowledge of the indictment

15. The type of information about the client which is MORE essential in probation case   15.____
records than in case records used in other fields of social work is

    A. an interpretation of the client and his situation
    B. accurate and easily available reference to verified facts about the client
    C. a running record of the progress of treatment
    D. a description of the client's attitude and reactions to his problems

16. A probation supervision case record generally includes all of the following EXCEPT   16.____

    A. contacts made with the probationer
    B. the probationer's personal and social situation

C.   the probationer's progress in treatment
D.   a copy of the original complaint

17. In writing case records, a probation officer should try to achieve a factual but interpretive   17._____
report that gives a true picture of an individual and his situation. Which one of the following BEST describes the approximate proportions of factual and interpretive material
which should be included in a typical case record?
_____ factual; _____ interpretive.

   A.   10%; 90%   B.   20%; 80%   C.   50%; 50%   D.   90%; 10%

18. Which one of the following represents the MOST acceptable and desirable method of   18._____
keeping case records?

   A.   Records should include face sheets which are complete and constantly updated,
        with opening summary and periodic progress reports.
   B.   Records should include full process recording and interpretation of the probation
        officer's thoughts and actions.
   C.   A periodic summary recording should be prepared to show case movement, with
        detailed recording at crisis spots.
   D.   Handwritten memoranda should be filed chronologically, covering the probationer's
        activities or the probation officer's reasoning at the time of writing.

19. A narrative record usually begins with a description of the complaint which brought the   19._____
offender to the Department of Probation and continues with a relevant history of the
case.
Of the following, the MAIN advantage of organizing materials in this manner is that it

   A.   indicates the basic reason why the offender is known to the criminal justice system
   B.   gives the presiding judge all the facts before making a disposition of the case
   C.   makes it easy for a new probation officer taking on the case in progress to learn all
        the facts readily
   D.   fulfills the requirement that law enforcement agencies follow this procedure

20. Which one of the following should NOT be an integral part of a narrative record?   20._____

   A.   A printed questionnaire, to record the probationer's responses and the probation
        officer's interpretive comments
   B.   A flexible structure, to allow for the nature of the situation and individuality of the
        probation officer
   C.   Records of interviews with the offender, family members, and witnesses to the
        offense
   D.   The probation officer's interpretation of the individual and the situation involved

21. The part of the pre-sentence report prepared by a probation officer which is MOST help-   21._____
ful for diagnostic and treatment purposes is the

   A.   face sheet   B.   study of the offense
   C.   arrest report   D.   social case study

Questions 22-25.

DIRECTIONS: Questions 22 through 25 are to be answered SOLELY on the basis of the fol-
              lowing statement.

The initial contact between the offender and the correctional social worker frequently occurs at the point of extreme crisis, when the usual adaptive mechanisms have been broken down. In many areas of correctional practice, such as probation and parole, this contact is often followed by long periods during which limited freedom is officially imposed. It is at such points that response to the offer of hope for restoring equilibrium may mean most, and that new coping capacities and new person-environment relationships develop. As a result, many correctional social workers have become skilled in strategies of crisis intervention. What they learn from such endeavors does not generally find its way into the professional literature; thus the correctional social worker has contributed little to developing and testing practice theory. However, beginning efforts are being made to remedy this situation, and it is probable that corrections may provide an important laboratory from which tomorrow's understanding of the theory and strategies of crisis intervention will emerge.

22. Which of the following is the MOST appropriate title for the above statement?   22.____

    A. Correctional Social Work in Crisis
    B. Crisis Intervention and Correctional Social Work
    C. Coping Capacities of Probationers and Parolees
    D. The Theory and Practice of Crisis Intervention

23. It can be concluded from the above statement that crisis intervention as a method of treatment and rehabilitation in correctional social work is based on the premise that a(n)   23.____

    A. offender may be more likely to respond to help and change his life style at a time of crisis, such as being on probation or parole, when incarceration is the only other alternative
    B. person is not likely to respond to help and change his life style unless he is in a crisis situation, such as being on probation or parole, when he is threatened by imprisonment
    C. offender sentenced to probation or parole is likely to respond to help and change his life style, because his freedom is limited and supervision is imposed on him
    D. situation such as probation or parole, in which an offender is supervised and his freedom is limited, presents ideal conditions for constructive personality change

24. On the basis of the above statement, it would be VALID to assume that   24.____

    A. offenders sentenced to probation and parole usually develop coping capacities which would not emerge during imprisonment
    B. offenders who are rehabilitated as a result of probation or parole have greater coping capacities in crisis situations
    C. a life crisis situation such as being sentenced to probation or parole may become a positive force toward an offender's rehabilitation
    D. an offender's ability to develop new coping capacities in times of crisis should be a decisive factor in determining the recommended sentence

25. According to the above statement, correctional social workers' experiences in crisis intervention have   25.____

    A. encouraged use of crisis intervention strategy
    B. contributed to theory rather than practice
    C. not resulted in further learning
    D. not generally been reported in print

KEY (CORRECT ANSWERS)

1.	B		11.	B
2.	B		12.	A
3.	C		13.	B
4.	C		14.	B
5.	A		15.	B
6.	C		16.	D
7.	B		17.	C
8.	B		18.	C
9.	B		19.	A
10.	B		20.	A

21.	D
22.	B
23.	A
24.	C
25.	D

———

TEST 2

DIRECTIONS: Each question or incomplete statement is followed by several suggested answers or completions. Select the one that BEST answers the question or completes the statement. *PRINT THE LETTER OF THE CORRECT ANSWER IN THE SPACE AT THE RIGHT.*

1. Of the following letters written to a probation department in another jurisdiction, which one is written in the MOST acceptable style?   1.____

    A. This department wishes to acknowledge your communication of the 17th regarding your officers' efforts to locate John Jones. We wish to thank you for your efforts and ask you to return the warrant. Please be assured that we will cooperate with you should the occasion arise.

    B. This is in reply to your letter of May 17th, in which you advise that your officers have made an extensive search for John Jones, without success. Please accept our expression of appreciation for your services, and feel free to return the warrant. If we can ever render like service, feel free to call on us.

    C. This is in reply to your letter of May 17th. We want to thank you for your extensive efforts to find our fugitive, John Jones. You may return the warrant to us. If we can ever give similar assistance to your department, please do not hesitate to get in touch with us.

    D. Your letter of May 17th is herewith acknowledged. We note that your officers have made an extensive effort to locate John Jones, without finding him. We deem it advisable to terminate the search at present, and request you to return the warrant to us. We stand ready to accommodate you should you ever require our service in like circumstances

2. Assume that, as a probation officer, you are working on the police record section of a pre-sentence investigation report on an offender who has been arrested ten times in the last five years on various charges. Despite follow-up, however, you are unable to determine the disposition of half of these cases. The deadline for your report is the next day. Which one of the following courses of action would it be MOST appropriate for you to take with regard to preparing this section of your report? List   2.____

    A. all the arrests and only those dispositions of which you are aware, and leave a blank space for the unknown dispositions

    B. all the arrests and dispositions on cases of which you are aware, and fill in *no response from FBI* or other appropriate remarks on the cases whose dispositions are unknown

    C. none of the arrests and dispositions, but include instead an explanatory statement regarding the unavailability of complete disposition data

    D. only those arrests for which there are dispositions available, and make an explanatory statement to the effect that other arrests and dispositions will be added to the report when the information becomes available

3. For purposes of establishing rapport and obtaining information, the relative importance of an interviewer's overt behavior during an interview as compared to his underlying attitudes is such that the interviewer's overt behavior is GENERALLY considered   3.____

    A. dependent on the client's attitudes and behavior
    B. of equal importance

    C.   less important
    D.   more important

4. *Summary jurisdiction* is CORRECTLY defined as the   4.____

    A.   authority of a court or magistrate to sentence defendants charged with minor offenses without indictment and usually without a jury
    B.   action of a court or magistrate in cancelling or terminating a probationary period either to discharge or sentence the probationer
    C.   recommittal of an accused person to custody after a partial or preliminary hearing before a judge or magistrate
    D.   notice or order requiring a person to appear before a court for the purpose of being arraigned on the charge of committing an offense

5. It is considered advisable for the probation officer to classify his caseload according to   5.____
the needs of his probationers and the kinds of service to be provided MAINLY because appropriate classification

    A.   gives the judge a reliable indication of the seriousness of the offense and the offender's problems
    B.   enables the probation officer to focus his attention and talents on areas of greatest need and potential product iveness
    C.   makes it unnecessary for agency representatives and other professionals involved in the case to read all details of the case record
    D.   indicates whether or not the probationer should be referred for psychiatric examination

6. The CHIEF distinction between a parolee and a probationer is that a parolee must have   6.____

    A.   already served a part of his sentence in a penal or reformative institution before being released
    B.   been placed on probation more than once within a 10-year period
    C.   been convicted of a civil rather than a criminal offense
    D.   been convicted of a felony rather than a misdemeanor

7. Children who have suffered from an attack of encephalitis sometimes become behavior   7.____
problems or develop abnormal personality traits and are classified as psychoneurotic. If such a child becomes part of your caseload, you, as a probation officer, should know that generally the MOST effective type of treatment is

    A.   probation   B.   foster home placement
    C.   penal   D.   medical

8. A probation officer would use a clearance from a social service exchange PRIMARILY to   8.____
obtain information on

    A.   a probationer's family background, including police records
    B.   a probationer's history of mental or physical treatment in public institutions
    C.   any other agencies previously having contact with a probationer
    D.   applications for public assistance by the probationer's family

9. In recommending a sentence of either probation or commitment to the court for a juvenile   9.____
offender, the one of the following which should be taken into consideration LEAST by a probation officer is

A. the offender's potential for rehabilitation
B. social situations which can be utilized at home
C. the offender's pledges to behave in the future
D. social situations which can be utilized in the offender's school

10. The legal written document which initiates a case in Family Court is GENERALLY referred to as a(n)   10.____

   A. charge   B. indictment
   C. petition   D. information

11. Assume that you, as a probation officer, have an adolescent girl in your caseload, who is a recent runaway.   11.____
   Of the following, the service agency you should contact FIRST to help locate the runaway girl would be

   A. Travelers Aid Society
   B. Juvenile Protective Association
   C. YWCA
   D. Salvation Army

12. When an offender is sentenced to probation, this sentence generally should NOT be interpreted as a   12.____

   A. form of mercy or leniency
   B. contract between the offender and the court
   C. process of treatment prescribed by the court
   D. conditional release of the offender

13. Of the following, the MOST important reason for utilizing the intake procedure for juveniles in Family Court whenever possible is to   13.____

   A. save time for the Department of Probation staff
   B. satisfy the petitioner or complainant
   C. prevent the profound psychological effect on juveniles of a court visit
   D. enable parents of juveniles to have a greater voice in disposition of cases

14. Studies have shown that the correlation between a defendant's educational and vocational adjustment patterns and his emotional and social stability is USUALLY   14.____

   A. zero   B. positive
   C. negative   D. curvilinear

15. The one of the following which is NOT a responsibility of intake, as an integral part of the probation process, is to   15.____

   A. provide the opportunity for a satisfactory adjustment without court action
   B. refer cases to community agencies whenever the need for social services is indicated
   C. provide extended services if necessary in order to adjust cases satisfactorily
   D. refer to court only those cases that require court action

16. Recent newspaper articles have discussed proposed controversial legislation to change   16._____
the minimum age at which a juvenile can be tried in criminal court instead of in family
court.
This proposed legislation is concerned SPECIFICALLY with _____ the age from

_____.

    A. lowering; 16 to 14   B. lowering; 18 to 16
    C. raising; 14 to 16   D. raising; 16 to 18

17. A recent study of the results of compulsory and voluntary referrals of alcoholic probation-   17._____
ers to psychotherapy indicates that those assigned to a compulsory treatment group had
a more successful period of probation than those assigned to a voluntary treatment
group. Probationers in compulsory treatment were in violation of probation for failure to
attend a single treatment session, while those in the voluntary group were required to
attend the first session only.
These data suggest that, in general,

    A. compulsion may be a necessary factor for motivation and successful treatment of
probationers
    B. initial motivation is a guarantee of successful treatment of probationers
    C. voluntary treatment of probationers results in decreased motivation
    D. successful treatment of probationers is directly related to their initial motivation to
participate

18. For which one of the following crimes may a sentence of probation NOT be given in the   18._____
state?

    A. Assault on a police officer
    B. Possession of a marijuana cigarette
    C. Grand larceny of over $100,000
    D. Possession of one ounce of heroin

19. Assume that one of your probationers appears for a scheduled appointment, admits that   19._____
he is addicted to narcotics, and asks for help.
As a probation officer, which one of the following would be the BEST action for you to
take FIRST for both the probationer's well-being and the protection of society?

    A. Arrest the probationer for illegal use of narcotics and prepare a charge of violation
of probation
    B. Arrange to refer the probationer to a suitable narcotics treatment resource for with-
drawal treatment and further therapy and aftercare
    C. Refer the probationer to a methadone clinic
    D. Notify the Police Department Narcotics Squad

20. The practice of disclosing information contained in pre-sentence reports to adult defen-   20._____
dants or their counsel is a controversial issue.
Of the following, the argument against disclosing pre-sentence reports to defendants
which is LEAST valid is that this practice would

    A. make it difficult for probation officers to obtain confidential information from other
agencies
    B. cause unreasonable delays, since defendants are able to challenge information in
the reports with which they disagree

    C.   be harmful to rehabilitative efforts, particularly in cases where psychiatric evaluations are included

    D.   reveal information about police techniques in apprehending criminal offenders

Questions 21-25.

DIRECTIONS: Questions 21 through 25 are to be answered SOLELY on the basis of the following statement.

The group worker must be concerned with two major goals in correctional treatment of juvenile offenders: (a) sustaining and reinforcing conventional value systems, and (b) enhancing the youth's positive self-image and general feeling of worthiness. The group processes involved in working toward these ends are so interrelated that treatment can meet both goals by improving interpersonal skills and experiences. As an initial concept, it is important to recognize that, in spite of delinquent behavior, adolescents usually do exhibit conscience formation, as may be seen in their support of conformity values, evidence of guilt and conventional behavior, and rationalization of delinquent behavior. It is this very ambivalence toward the conventional order that can be the basis for rehabilitation. On the basis of the distinction between real guilt and guilt reflecting emotional problems, an ideal therapeutic objective is to reach the point at which the internal and external controls are in general harmony and agency expectations are closely allied to and consistent with group and individual expectations.

21.   Which of the following is the BEST title for the above statement?   21.____

    A.   Group Treatment of Juvenile Offenders
    B.   The Group Worker and Correctional Treatment
    C.   The Juvenile Offender
    D.   Conscience Formation in Juvenile Offenders

22.   On the basis of the above statement, it would be VALID to assume that group treatment   22.____
   of the juvenile offender can result in the development of

    A.   greater self-confidence
    B.   rationalization of delinquent behavior
    C.   guilt and conscience formation
    D.   increased conscientiousness

23.   On the basis of the above statement, it would be VALID to conclude that juvenile offend-   23.____
   ers

    A.   are anxious for rehabilitation
    B.   have no internal or external controls
    C.   are deficient in interpersonal skills and experiences
    D.   feel more guilt because of emotional problems than because of offenses committed

24.   According to the above statement, a characteristic of juvenile offenders which makes   24.____
   them amenable to correctional treatment is that they

    A.   can be reached by group processes
    B.   have a general feeling of worthiness
    C.   show signs of conscience formation
    D.   are ambivalent toward rehabilitation

25. According to the above statement, an IDEAL therapeutic objective in the group treatment 25.____
of juvenile offenders would be based on

    A. agency expectations
    B. group expectations
    C. the distinction between real guilt and irrational guilt
    D. the harmony between external and internal controls

_____

KEY (CORRECT ANSWERS)

1.	C		11.	A
2.	B		12.	A
3.	D		13.	C
4.	A		14.	B
5.	B		15.	C
6.	A		16.	A
7.	D		17.	A
8.	C		18.	D
9.	C		19.	B
10.	C		20.	D

21.	A
22.	A
23.	C
24.	C
25.	C

_____

EXAMINATION SECTION
TEST 1

DIRECTIONS: Each question or incomplete statement is followed by several suggested answers or completions. Select the one that BEST answers the question or completes the statement. *PRINT THE LETTER OF THE CORRECT ANSWER IN THE SPACE AT THE RIGHT.*

1. The philosophy of case work is based upon the   1.____

    A. recognition of the dignity of the human person
    B. place of the agency in the community
    C. importance of planning realistically with clients
    D. role of the worker in case work treatment

2. Social case work aims CHIEFLY to   2.____

    A. give material assistance and help the client achieve success
    B. find the reasons for the person's difficulty and refer him for help to the proper source
    C. help the person through a professional relationship to gain a better understanding of his problem and to help him make a satisfactory adjustment
    D. improve the person's environment

3. The interview in case work is used CHIEFLY   3.____

    A. to get proof of data required in evaluating the client's problems and resources
    B. as a tool to explore with the client his feelings about his problem, as well as about the problem itself, so as to arrive at a plan of treatment
    C. because it is less expensive than other methods of work
    D. for statistical purposes on the basis of the worker's record

4. The case work relationship between the worker and the client is important CHIEFLY because it   4.____

    A. is a friendly relationship which the client needs at times
    B. provides an opportunity for the client to talk things out
    C. is a professional relationship to which the worker brings specific knowledge and skills to help another person
    D. provides concentrated attention to problems over a short period of time

5. The case worker, to be MOST effective in helping another person, must   5.____

    A. be free from prejudice of any kind
    B. have a wide knowledge of the individual's cultural background
    C. have received help himself in order to better understand the client's feelings
    D. be aware as much as possible about his own feelings regarding his client

6. One of the BEST known marks of the mature person is the ability to   6.____

    A. control his feelings in difficult situations
    B. defer future pleasures or gratifications for long-term goals
    C. take things as they come, trusting in luck
    D. enjoy a great many outside interests in life

7. An adult with a mental age of 9 years was regarded psychologically as   7.____

    A. of normal mentality   B. a moron
    C. an imbecile   D. an idiot

8. The one of the following conditions which bears NO causative relationship to mental defi-   8.____
ciency is

    A. heredity   B. cerebral defect
    C. early postnatal trauma   D. dementia

9. Physical conditions which are caused by emotional conflicts are GENERALLY referred to   9.____
as being

    A. psycho-social   B. hypochondriacal
    C. psychosomatic   D. psychotic

10. Of the following conditions, the one in which anxiety is NOT generally found is   10.____

    A. psychopathic personality
    B. mild hysteria
    C. psychoneurosis
    D. compulsive-obsessive personality

11. Kleptomania may BEST be described as a   11.____

    A. neurotic drive to accumulate personal property through compulsive acts in order to
       dispose of it to others with whom one wishes friendship
    B. type of neurosis which manifests itself in an uncontrollable impulse to steal without
       economic motivation
    C. psychopathic trait which is probably hereditary in nature
    D. manifestation of punishment-inviting behavior based upon guilt feelings for some
       other crime or wrongdoing, fantasied or real, committed as a child

12. The one of the following tests which is NOT ordinarily used as a projective technique is   12.____
the

    A. Wechsler Bellevue Scale
    B. Rorschach Test
    C. Thematic Apperception Test
    D. Jung Free Association Test

13. An outstanding personality test in use at the present time is the Rorschach Test.   13.____
Of the following considerations, the GREATEST value of this test to the psychiatrist
and social worker is that it

    A. provides practical recommendations with reference to further educational and
       vocational training possibilities for the person tested
    B. reveals in quick, concise form the hereditary factors affecting the individual person-
       ality
    C. helps in substantiating a diagnosis of juvenile delinquency
    D. helps in a diagnostic formulation and in determining differential treatment

14. Of the following, the one through which ethical values are MOST generally acquired is   14.____

    A. heredity
    B. early training in school
    C. admonition and strict corrective measures by parents and other supervising adults
    D. integration into the self of parental values and attitudes

15. Records show that MOST crimes in the United States are committed by persons _____   15.____
years of age.

    A. under 18   B. from 18 to 25
    C. from 30 to 40   D. above 40

16. According to current theories of criminology, the one of the following which is regarded as   16.____
the MOST important cause of delinquency is

    A. personality maladjustment
    B. lack of proper housing
    C. mental deficiency
    D. community indifference to the need for recreational facilities

17. Delinquent behavior is MOST generally a result of   17.____

    A. living and growing up in an environment that is both socially and financially
        deprived
    B. a lack of educational opportunity for development of individual skills
    C. multiple factors - psychological, bio-social, emotional, and environmental
    D. low frustration tolerance of many parents toward problems of married life

18. Unmarried mothers USUALLY   18.____

    A. come from homes of poor economic status
    B. have had poor moral training in their youth
    C. are amoral or have little or no feeling of guilt
    D. all of the above

19. Alcoholism in the United States is USUALLY caused by   19.____

    A. the sense of frustration in one's work
    B. inadequacy of recreational facilities
    C. neurotic conflicts expressed in drinking excessively
    D. shyness and timidity

20. The MOST distinctive characteristic of the chronic alcoholic is that he drinks alcohol   20.____

    A. socially   B. compulsively
    C. periodically   D. secretly

21. *The chronic alcoholic is the person who cannot face reality without alcohol, and yet*   21.____
whose adequate adjustment to reality is impossible so long as he uses alcohol.
On the basis of this quotation, it is MOST reasonable to conclude that individuals over-
indulge in alcohol because alcohol

A. deadens the sense of conflict, giving the individual an illusion of social competence and a feeling of well-being and success
B. provides the individual with an outlet to display his feelings of good-fellowship and cheerfulness which are characteristic of his extroverted personality
C. affords an escape technique from habitual irrational fears, but does not affect rational fears
D. offers an escape from imagery and feelings of superiority which cause tension and anxiety

22. The one of the following drugs to which a person is LEAST likely to become addicted is   22.___

    A. opium   B. morphine   C. marijuana   D. heroin

23. Teenagers who become addicted to the use of drugs are MOST generally   23.___

    A. mentally defective   B. paranoid
    C. normally adventurous   D. emotionally disturbed

24. In the light of the current high rate of addiction to drugs among youths throughout the   24.___
    country, the one of the following statements which is generally considered to be LEAST
    correct is that

    A. a relatively large number of children and youths who experiment with drugs become addicts
    B. youths who use narcotics do so because of some emotional and personality disturbance
    C. youthful addicts are found largely among those who suffer to an abnormal extent deprivations in their personal development and growth
    D. the great majority of youthful addicts have had unfortunate home experiences and practically no contact with established community agencies

25. The Social Service Exchange is utilized by probation officers PRIMARILY in order to   25.___

    A. facilitate the operation of the Interstate Compact for the transfer of probationers
    B. secure a complete criminal record of the defendant awaiting sentence
    C. secure a listing of agencies which have known the defendant or his family
    D. acquire a developmental history of the defendant

Questions 26-32.

DIRECTIONS: Column I lists terms and Column II gives definitions.For each term listed in Column I, select its definition from Column II, and write the letter which precedes this definition.

<u>COLUMN I</u>

<u>COLUMN II</u>

26.   acquittal

A.   surrender by one state of a person found in that state for prosecution in another state having jurisdiction to try the charge

26._____

27.   arrest

B.   an official summons or notice to a person to appear before a court

27._____

28.   citation

C.   the act of taking a person into custody by authority of law

28._____

29.   commitment

D.   a formal written statement charging one or more persons with an offense as formulated by the prosecutor and found by a grand jury

29._____

30.   indictment

E.   bringing the accused before a court to answer a minimal charge

30._____

31.   recidivism

F.   an accusation of any offense or unlawful state of affairs originating with a grand jury from their own knowledge or observation

31._____

32.   rendition

G.   consignment to a place of official confinement of a person found guilty of a crime

32._____

H.   finding the accused not guilty of a crime after trial

I.   agreement to appear in court upon request, with-out bond

J.   reversion or relapse into prior criminal habits even after punishment

33. According to the statutes, a misdemeanor is an offense   33.____

    A. which is punishable by not more than an indeterminate term of from two to four years in a state prison
    B. not accompanied by physical violence
    C. for which reformatory sentence is mandatory unless sentence is suspended
    D. punishable by not more than one year of imprisonment

34. A person who is found guilty of a misdemeanor in a court may be kept under probation-   34.____
ary supervision for

    A. a maximum of one year
    B. a period not to exceed one-half of the prison term prescribed by law
    C. a maximum of three years
    D. as long as the court desires

35. According to the State Griminal Procedure Law, the period of probation in the case of a   35.____
child may NOT extend beyond

    A. his minority
    B. three years from the date of disposition
    C. the maximum time for which he might have been institutionalized
    D. the time required for him to make an adequate adjustment

36. According to the Criminal Procedure Law, the court which imposed the conditions of pro-   36.____
bation may

    A. not change them under any circumstances
    B. subsequently modify these conditions
    C. revise them only after one year of probation
    D. revise but not increase them

37. In cases of adult offenders, probation differs from parole in that probation involves   37.____

    A. suspension of sentence
    B. supervision after imprisonment
    C. supervision as a preliminary to parole
    D. un unlimited period of surveillance

38. One of the duties of the probation officer during pre-sentence investigations and the   38.____
supervision process is the consideration of evidence.
Of the following statements relating to the different types of evidence, the one which is
LEAST accurate is that

    A. real evidence consists of any facts which are secured by first-hand experience
    B. testimonial evidence is the assertion of a human being
    C. hearsay evidence has little or no validity in probation practice
    D. expert evidence is the testimony of a person with specialized knowledge of or skill in a particular field

39. *The effect of rumors may be temporary or lasting. If they are reinforced and if there is no appreciable conflict with other and then with newer impulses, they are likely to persist. The rumor-engendered impression, moreover, is often the first reaction to an event. Subsequent information labors under a psychological handicap even when it is perceived. If a man is ruined by lies which people have the desire to believe, only compelling truths can resurrect him. The truths, though, will not be responded to eagerly, and they most probably will not drive out all the effects from the past.*
Of the following, the statement which is MOST accurate on the basis of the above paragraph is that

    A. rumor-engendered impressions are readily obliterated if disproved by compelling truths
    B. uninformed rumors should not be spread since they usually ruin people's lives
    C. false rumors are disproved with difficulty, and the first impression of uncontested and disproved false rumors is likely to continue
    D. unlike the normal reaction to the rumor proved false, there is a psychological handicap in accepting the uncontested rumor

39._____

40. Of the following, the MAIN reason for keeping a case record in probation or parole supervision is to

    A. present a verified picture of all legal aspects of the case
    B. provide a complete and objective understanding of the person through knowledge gained from relatives, friends, and other agencies
    C. improve the quality of service to the probationer and to help the probation officer to understand him and his situation
    D. give a realistic picture of the employment and recreational activities of the person in order to evaluate his progress toward rehabilitation

40._____

KEY (CORRECT ANSWERS)

1. A	11. B	21. A	31. J
2. C	12. A	22. C	32. A
3. B	13. D	23. D	33. D
4. C	14. D	24. A	34. C
5. D	15. B	25. C	35. A
6. A	16. A	26. H	36. B
7. B	17. C	27. C	37. A
8. D	18. D	28. B	38. C
9. C	19. C	29. G	39. C
10. A	20. B	30. D	40. C

TEST 2

DIRECTIONS: Each question or incomplete statement is followed by several suggested answers or completions. Select the one that BEST answers the question or completes the statement. *PRINT THE LETTER OF THE CORRECT ANSWER IN THE SPACE AT THE RIGHT.*

1. The MOST accurate of the following statements concerning probation case records is that they

    A. are generically different from those in use in the private case work field
    B. differ radically from the procedural records of the court
    C. should of necessity place less emphasis on the treatment than on the investigation of a person on probation
    D. should emphasize surveillance factors of probation

1.____

2. Of the following reasons for maintaining records in the probation department, the one which has the LEAST significance to the agency and the probation officer is that

    A. case recording is an essential adjunct to the practice of case work
    B. accurate and current case records facilitate treatment
    C. case records represent the agency's knowledge, insight, experience, efforts, and plans in individual situations
    D. case records represent evidence with which to deny false accusations and derogatory evaluative statements arising in the community

2.____

3. The method of case recording which reflects the interaction between the client and the social worker around the problem as the client sees it and feels about it is known as

    A. chronological   B. process
    C. summary   D. topical

3.____

4. The one of the following which is the MOST important asset for a probation officer is

    A. a well-integrated personality
    B. expert knowledge of crime causation
    C. comprehensive knowledge of community resources
    D. good health to enable the office to cope with the hazards of probation work

4.____

5. A probation officer, newly assigned as a worker in a legalistic agency structure, must set goals for himself as a learner in a new experience.
The one of the following which MOST comprehensively and clearly states the learning goals of the new probation officer is to gain

    A. a comprehensive knowledge of the basic structure of the agency and the laws under which it operates
    B. a clear understanding of the objectives of the programs of the agency and of the underlying philosophy which governs the manner in which these programs are administered
    C. the integration of knowledge, development of skills in practice and growth in personal emotional structure necessary to enable him to help others most effectively
    D. the ability to recognize distress and signs of emotional disturbance in people and to treat symptomatic behavior while working within the agency framework

5.____

6.   The one of the following statements which is LEAST accurate is: 6._____

   A.   The type of evidence available in making a diagnosis of a person under investiga-
        tion by a probation officer generally is not of a probative value equal to that of facts
        found in the exact sciences
   B.   The rehabilitative treatment of a probationer lacks the precision used in treating
        physical diseases
   C.   The vast background of experience in probation work today makes it possible for
        the probation officer to diagnose with certainty the personality and character of the
        probationer
   D.   In considering evidence during an investigation, the probation officer can never be
        sure whether some fact has been overlooked that might alter the entire analysis

7.   The MOST accurate of the following statements with respect to reciprocal state legisla-   7._____
     tion to compel the support of dependent wives and children, better known as the Uniform
     Support of Dependents Law, is:

   A.   The amount of support allotted to women and children has been made uniform
        throughout the United States
   B.   Provision has been made for the deserted wife to make the complaint in the state
        of residence and for the order of support against her husband to be made in the
        state where her husband now resides
   C.   Sufficient federal funds have been provided to make it possible for the deserted
        wife to travel to the state where the deserting husband has been located and there
        make the proper complaint for support
   D.   The legal requirements of extradition concerning deserting husbands have been
        eased, thereby facilitating their return to the state where the spouse resides to face
        appropriate criminal action

8.   The one of the following statements which contains the basic principle upon which   8._____
     Aggressive Case Work GENERALLY operates is:

   A.   When a client applies for help with a delinquent child, the worker, following a com-
        plete study of the problem, forcefully and very definitely defines the solution of the
        problem to the client
   B.   The social worker waits until the neglect of a child by his parents reaches a point
        where the court should take action and then proceeds to remove the child from his
        home
   C.   New social work techniques are used to arouse the client's interest so that he vol-
        untarily requests aid
   D.   The social worker goes out to meet the client in his own setting

9.   Treatment of the delinquent child must be based on the child's individual needs PRIMA-   9._____
     RILY because

   A.   the child's needs are usually for adequate recreational facilities and better home
        conditions
   B.   social treatment depends upon social diagnosis, and sound diagnosis requires
        knowledge of the person
   C.   behavior is usually determined by environment, which is unique for each person
   D.   the child's needs are usually less complicated than those of an adult

10. It has been said that the probation officer working with a delinquent child *becomes for the*   10.____
child the symbol of the authority against which he rebels. The task of the probation officer
is to convert what appears to be a handicap into an asset.
Of the following approaches to this problem, the one which serves the probation officer
MOST advantageously is to

    A. disguise his role of authority by becoming a friend to the child, who will then
respond in a more personal way by talking freely about himself and his experiences
    B. strengthen the parents so that they will relax their parental authoritative role and be
more permissive in their discipline of the child
    C. maintain his authority while offering guidance and counsel on the basis of disci-
plined concern for the child, genuine warmth, and willingness and capacity to enter
into his feelings and thinking about persons, situations, and things
    D. refer the case to an agency in the community where the non-authoritative setting
will permit reaching the child on a social and psychological basis through the use
of treatment techniques for emotionally disturbed children

11. Of the following statements relating to probation of known alcoholics, the one which is   11.____
MOST accurate is:

    A. In order to help an alcoholic person under supervision, a probation officer should
consider it important for the family to understand something of the probationer's
problem
    B. Referral of alcoholic probationers to medical facilities for the administration of cer-
tain drugs has proven successful in practically all cases
    C. Research to date demonstrates that, in general, alcoholics on probation make an
easy and adequate adjustment
    D. Most domestic relations problems are caused by alcoholics or heavy drinkers

12. Probation officers frequently encounter problems of young adults, either single or mar-   12.____
ried, with deep, unresolved dependency conflicts who cannot make mature adjustments
in their work, living arrangements, or handling of their marital and parent-child relationships. The one of the following which is MOST appropriate in case work with individuals
or families presenting problems of this type is

    A. environment service, affording immediate adjustments of an external character
    B. specific advice and concrete suggestions given directly by the case worker upon
his own initiative
    C. case work treatment through which the person learns to handle his situation realis-
tically with lessened anxiety as a result of a clearer understanding of deep-seated,
repressed emotional material
    D. supportive counseling in helping the person to gain some beginning insight into his
basic problem so that he can be helped, if need is indicated, to move on to psychiatric treatment

13. In supervising an unemployed probationer, the one of the following actions which ordi-   13.____
narily represents GOOD probation practice is to

    A. refer the probationer immediately to the State Unemployment Bureau
    B. encourage the probationer and give him supportive help in using his own initiative
to secure employment

C. refer the probationer to personal employer contacts known to the probation officer
D. fix a time limit for the probationer to get a job before returning him to court for violation of probation

14. The majority of cases coming to a court because of marital discord are presented at a time of crisis.
Of the following approaches, the one which is MOST essential to the probation officer in offering help to a family in this situation is

    14.____

  A. early analysis of his own attitudes and reactions in differentiating between factors already present in the personalities of the husband and wife and of situational factors
  B. immediate determination of the legal aspects of the marriage problem and recognition and handling of transference and counter-transference in the case work relationship
  C. establishing of a relationship which will enable the client to express his feelings and to present the problem as he sees it, thus enabling the probation officer to arrive at a sound diagnostic judgment
  D. offering of a relationship at a level that will provide a vent to the husband and wife, endeavoring to use psychological support to direct them towards reconciliation

15. Mr. X, while on probation on a charge of desertion, again absconds, leaving his family without provision for support. The one of the following actions to be taken FIRST by the probation officer in apprehending the probationer is to

    15.____

  A. file a probation warrant with the local police department
  B. prepare a violation of probation report requesting the court to issue a bench warrant
  C. request the court to revoke the man's probation and advise his wife to immediately make a new complaint of desertion
  D. interview the deserted wife in order to understand her feelings about her husband's desertion and to discuss with her, if she wishes, the possible whereabouts of the probationer

16. A boy of 15, on probation for one year in the Children's Court on an original petition of delinquency made by his inadequate mother, has shown no improvement in his behavior, is beyond her control, and is associating with a gang consisting of other seriously delinquent boys.
Of the following courses of action, the one which is MOST advisable for the probation officer to pursue is to

    16.____

  A. refer the boy for psychiatric evaluation or recommendation to determine whether he should be committed to an institution where he might receive treatment in a controlled environment
  B. refer the family to a social agency for counseling to improve the home situation
  C. arrange to have more frequent interviews with the mother
  D. caution the boy that unless he improves his behavior and disassociates himself from the gang, the probation officer will be forced to recommend commitment to an institution

17. An adolescent girl held as a material witness in a case of rape expresses strong hostility   17.____
towards her mother, whom she claims always favored her younger brother. The mother
says, in an interview, that she was always devoted to her own mother, now deceased, but
that she was never able to confide in her or feel that she was understood by her. This
knowledge of the mother's earlier experiences may provide a clue to the probation officer
in understanding causative factors in the girl's behavior.
Of the following explanations, the one which MOST likely accounts for the poor relationship between mother and daughter is that the

    A. mother's greater interest in and warmth for her son would indicate that she had a
better relationship with her own father than with her mother
    B. mother of the girl had lacked a warm, trusting relationship with her own mother
and, therefore, provided an overpermissive atmosphere in her home for her daughter, believing that this would create a closer relationship between them
    C. girl's behavior springs from a fantasied maturity which is a spurious and unreal
assumption of an adult status, often a temporary phase in adolescent growth
    D. mother of the girl probably had not worked through problems in relationship with
her own mother and was unable, therefore, to establish a sound relationship with
her daughter

18. A girl of 19, adjudicated as a wayward minor and placed on probation, is discovered by   18.____
the probation officer to be a prostitute, although this has not yet come to the attention of
the authorities.
The one of the following courses of action which is MOST advisable for the probation
officer to pursue in these circumstances is to

    A. recommend that probation be revoked and that the girl be committed to an institu-
tion
    B. advise the girl that unless she discontinues this behavior the probation officer will
have to report it to the court
    C. give the girl an opportunity to work out the problem for herself
    D. re-evaluate the case, discussing the matter with the probation officer's supervisor
and determining appropriate action to take for the best interests of the community
and the probationer

19. Mrs. A comes to a social agency asking for help with her 8-year-old son who is a truant   19.____
from school and is generally willful and disobedient. Mr. A travels a good deal and is seldom at home. He has had very little part in the rearing of the child.
Of the following actions, the one which the case worker should take FIRST is to

    A. see the child in order to learn from him why he is misbehaving
    B. arrange to see the father in order to advise him to change his job
    C. explore with Mr. A her feelings about the child as well as her feelings about her
husband's part in the family picture
    D. visit the school to discover the cause of the difficulty there

20. A 17-year-old male on probation in the Family Court tells his probation officer that he   20.____
resents reporting to him because he was innocent of the crime for which he was placed
on probation. In addition, he states he dislikes the probation officer.
In this situation, the one of the following courses of action which the probation officer
should pursue is to

A. encourage the probationer to seek legal assistance to reopen the case
B. adopt a firm attitude indicating that he is not interested in the probationer's guilt or innocence and insisting that he comply with the probation conditions
C. seek to understand the reasons why the probationer dislikes him, at the same time indicating to him that he is free to explore legal assistance regarding his original offense
D. consider the probationer as rebellious and a potential community threat, recommending that probation be revoked

21. *A person's behavior is both shaped and judged by the expectations he and his culture have invested in his status and the major social roles he carries.*
According to this principle, a caseworker can BEST make effective professional judgments and plan proper treatment if he recognizes that   21._____

A. the client's problem may stem from role conflicts
B. the client faces difficulties serenely once he knows what society expects of him
C. cultural values have little to do with a client's status
D. the status-seeking individual is not able to comprehend the function of cultural values in his life

22. The diagnostic approach in social casework, often called the Freudian School, has as its basic premise the   22._____

A. investigation of past events of the client's life experiences and functioning in order to understand his present situation
B. study of the subconscious mind of the client as to his present attitude and understanding about his situation
C. examination of behavioral motivation of the client
D. solution of the client's problem through aptitude testing and group therapy

23. There is implicit in casework an acceptance of a client's value system which may be different from that of the caseworker.
Of the following, the MOST valid conclusion to be derived from this statement is that   23._____

A. clients do not have moral standards
B. the caseworkers' standards are always stricter than the clients' standards
C. cultural patterns have little effect on value systems by either clients or caseworkers
D. a caseworker has no right to insist on conformity of a client's behavior with his own standards

24. The establishment and maintenance of a professional relationship with a client is stressed in casework. This relationship should be   24._____

A. clear, business-like, and delimited by the agency function
B. permissive, friendly, and kindly, with the pace determined by the client
C. warm, enabling, and consciously controlled by the caseworker
D. variable and unpredictable because of the fluctuations in client need

25. There is great interest being shown currently in the possible merger of the child welfare and family casework fields, in private as well as public agencies.
The BEST argument in support of such a merger is that   25._____

    A. families with child care problems would not be broken up through placement of children
    B. the taxpayer's and the voluntary contributor's money would be saved
    C. through intensive work with children, prevention of the development of behavior problems would be possible
    D. new techniques in family casework treatment and the development of new community resources would probably result

26. Family casework involves working with parents and children about problems involving maintenance and survival.
Of the following types of problems, the MOST important one that a family caseworker has to handle generally involves
    26.____

    A. relationships between siblings
    B. budgeting
    C. psychotherapeutic problems
    D. environmental deficiencies

27. The authoritative approach in casework, also known as aggressive casework, essentially involves
    27.____

    A. the breakup of families whose members no longer get along together
    B. purposeful, persistent casework methods observing respect for the individual
    C. direct supervision of a family until their problems are resolved
    D. the application of techniques evolved by law enforcement agencies to social casework

28. The term ambivalence, as used in social casework, might BEST be illustrated by the
    28.____

    A. inability of the client to follow the recommendations of the caseworker, due to his own unresolved conflicts
    B. presentation to the client of more than one reasonable course of action for the client to follow
    C. client's lack of any knowledge of how to solve his problem
    D. client's fears for his future welfare

29. There is general agreement among experts in the field that, when dealing with a client or handling a case, a caseworker should
    29.____

    A. place emphasis on the objective aspects, directing her work primarily to the physical factors in the client that indicate need for change
    B. place emphasis on the environmental factors, especially those surrounding the client which have caused him to be in his present state
    C. give attention not only to the environmental factors and social experiences, but also the client's feelings about, and reactions to, his experience
    D. consider each factor in the case as a separate unit after carefully distinguishing between the truly environmental and the truly emotional factors

30. In casework practice, the unit of attention is generally considered to be the family, although in some agencies the client or patient is often viewed as being outside of his family.
The trend in modern casework with respect to the family of a client is to
    30.____

A. involve the family wherever feasible in the total casework process
B. scientifically determine wherein the family is harmful to the client and try to make plans for the client to leave his family
C. educate the public so that families of clients will not interfere with agency plans
D. refer every member of the family for casework help

31. John L., 15, was referred to a youth counseling agency by the principal of the high school he attends because he has been truanting for the past six months. He is of above average intelligence, is in his sophomore year, and is currently failing 4 out of 5 of his courses. His mother says that he frequently comes home after midnight and is friendly with two boys with court records. The family group consists of John and his mother, who supports them by working as a secretary. The sisters, 19 and 21, are married and out of the home. Mr. L. deserted when John was 3. The principal told John he had to go to the youth counseling agency or be brought into court by the truant officer.
   In beginning to work with John, the caseworker should FIRST

   A. recognize that since John did not come voluntarily, he will refuse casework treatment
   B. establish himself as an adult who will keep John in line
   C. secure more facts about John and his situation in order to determine further case activity
   D. promise that the agency will keep John from being sent to juvenile court

31._____

32. A client tells the social worker that he is planning to leave his job as a junior executive trainee in a department store for a job as a laborer which will pay him a higher salary. After exploring the client's reasons for making this move, the caseworker feels the plan is unwise since the trainee position offers a considerably better future.
   In this situation, it would be BEST for the caseworker to

   A. attempt to dissuade the client from making the job change, pointing out the reasons for the inadvisability of the move
   B. allow the client to change jobs, without attempting to dissuade or counsel him
   C. refuse to give the client permission to change jobs, without an attempt to dissuade or counsel him
   D. try to dissuade the client from making the job change without giving the real reasons for thinking the move undesirable

32._____

33. Casework interviewing is always directed to the client and his situation.
   The one of the following which is the MOST accurate statement with respect to the proper focus of an interview is that the

   A. caseworker limits the client to concentration on objective data
   B. client is generally permitted to talk about facts and feelings with no direction from the caseworker
   C. main focus in casework interviews is on feelings rather than facts
   D. caseworker is responsible for helping the client focus on any material which seems to be related to his problems or difficulties

33._____

34. A recent development in casework interviewing procedure, known as multiple-client inter-   34.____
    viewing, consists of interviews of the entire family at the same time. However, this may
    not be an effective casework method in certain situations.
    Of the following, the situation in which the standard individual interview would be
    PREFERABLE is when

    A. family members derive consistent and major gratification from assisting each other
       in their destructive responses
    B. there is a crucial family conflict to which the members are reacting
    C. the family is overwhelmed by interpersonal anxieties which have not been explored
    D. the worker wants to determine the pattern of family interaction to further his diag-
       nostic understanding

35. The one of the following which is the CHIEF value of verbatim recording of all or a portion   35.____
    of an important interview is the possibility it offers for

    A. careful study and clarification of psychological goals in treatment
    B. a prompt solution to the problem by preservation, in an orderly and concise fash-
       ion, of the full psychological and economic picture of the client's situation
    C. quick determination of the more obvious social goals and offering of concrete ser-
       vices by presentation of the essential facts
    D. supervision of experienced workers by showing the emotional overtones, subtle
       reactions, and intricate worker-client interchanges

36. Experts in the field of social casework recording generally agree that the kind of case   36.____
    material for which the narrative form of recording is MOST suitable is

    A. material that deals with feelings, attitudes, and client-worker relationships because
       this style permits the use of primary evidence in the form of verbal material and
       behavior observed in the interview
    B. social data, including eligibility material and family background history, because it
       can then be presented in a chronological, orderly fashion to enable the worker to
       select the desired facts
    C. personal facts concerning the individual's personality patterns and their growth and
       development because they can be seen in an orderly progression from primal
       immaturity until their ultimate stage of completion
    D. selectively chosen and documented material essential to a quicker and clearer
       understanding of the various ramifications of the case by a new worker, when
       responsibility for handling the client is reassigned

37. A case record includes relevant social and psychological facts about the client, the   37.____
    nature of his request, his feeling about his situation, his attitude towards the agency, and
    his use of and reaction to treatment.
    In addition, it should ALWAYS contain

    A. routine history
    B. complete details of personality development and emotional relationships
    C. detailed process accounts of all contacts
    D. data necessary for understanding the problem and the factors important in arriving
       at a solution

38. The CHIEF basis for the inability of a troubled client to express his problem clearly to the caseworker is that the client   38.____

    A. sees his problem in complex terms and does not think it possible to give the caseworker the whole picture
    B. has erected defenses against emotions that seem to him inadmissible or intolerable
    C. cannot describe how he feels about his problem
    D. views the situation as unlikely to be solved and is blocked in self-expression

39. During his pre-sentence investigation, a defendant gave information about his participation in the offense which conflicted with the official version. He was placed on probation. Now the district attorney wishes to use him as a witness against a co-defendant and asks for permission to use the pre-sentence report as a basis for cross-examination. Of the following, the BEST course of action to take is to   39.____

    A. refuse to turn over the report on the ground that the report is the property of the court and its contents cannot be revealed without authority of the court
    B. turn over the report to the district attorney but caution him to hold the source of his information confidential
    C. refer the request to the Director of Probation on the ground that this involves policy which no one else is ever authorized to handle
    D. advise the district attorney's office that the entire report cannot be sent to him but portions of it may be discussed with his representative

40. During the course of a pre-sentence investigation, the defendant reveals certain details of the offense not previously known and involves others who have not been apprehended.
Of the following, the FIRST action to be taken by the probation officer on the case is to   40.____

    A. discuss the matter with the chief probation officer, asking guidance on methods of procedure
    B. report the new information to the district attorney's office immediately
    C. withhold the information until it can be disclosed to the court through the pre-sentence report in order to let the court decide how it is to be used
    D. advise the client of the importance of this information and ask him if he is prepared to make the same disclosures to the district attorney

41. A young man on probation after an offense involving fraudulent checks and impersonation of an officer is given work at a hospital as an attendant. Within three weeks, he marries a nurse's aide. A full investigation discloses that he told her he was wealthy, of good family, working humbly to *prove* himself.
Of the following, the FIRST action for the probation officer to take in this case is to   41.____

    A. secure a warrant and cause his arrest immediately
    B. check with the hospital to get other details
    C. attempt to analyze the behavior pattern for causative factors
    D. recommend that the young couple get an annulment

42. The wife of a former probationer telephones the probation office stating that her husband has disappeared and she is anxious to secure all possible leads in order to aid the police in looking for him.
Of the following, the BEST reply to be made to her is that   42.____

A. this is a job for the police, but if there are any developments, she will be informed
B. the case is closed and no help can be given her
C. she should consult her religious advisor and her attorney
D. the husband has had numerous previous girlfriends to whom he might have returned

43. A person of foreign birth is placed on probation but understands little English and cannot read or write. Of the following, the MOST appropriate action is to   43.____

    A. order him to attend night classes in English
    B. direct him to obtain someone who speaks his language to interpret the condition of probation
    C. encourage him to seek language training and tell him that his probation will be revoked if he shows unwillingness to overcome his language handicap
    D. give him guidance in finding a language class which will fit his needs and situation

44. The probation officer who made the pre-sentence investigation on a certain case happens to be personally acquainted with the judge who imposed sentence. Some time later, the judge receives a letter from the sentenced prisoner. The judge asks the probation officer to investigate this letter and make a recommendation.
Of the following, the BEST action for the probation officer to take is to   44.____

    A. make the investigation and report directly to the judge
    B. ask the judge to speak to his superior about this assignment
    C. complete the report and submit it to his superior for approval without prior consultation with the latter
    D. report to his superior that he has had a request for a supplementary investigation and await his decision as to whether it should be assigned to him or another officer

45. Having read another agency's record for information, it is GOOD case reporting practice to   45.____

    A. quote the agency worker as the source of information and include any pertinent opinions given in the agency file
    B. identify the source and report it over your signature as a part of the record
    C. use the words *it is alleged* or *according to a reliable source* or *we have been informed*
    D. refer to the other agency as Confidential Source No. 1, etc.

46. The type of pre-sentence report which is of GREATEST value is one which contains   46.____

    A. a diagnostic interpretation of the etiology of the offense
    B. the essential facts and indicates the treatment needs of the defendant
    C. the essential facts about the defendant
    D. a supplemental psychiatric study

47. The LEAST important reason for a probation officer to make a pre-sentence investigation and report is to   47.____

    A. assist the judge in making proper disposition of the case
    B. find conditions within the family which need the services of other agencies

C. assist the probation officer who will supervise the defendant if he is placed on probation

D. provide a case record for the institution if the defendant is committed

48. The one of the following statements which is MOST accurate in regard to violation of probation is that a violator should be returned to court   48._____

   A. only if he is guilty of a serious violation
   B. if further use of the authority of the court will have a therapeutic value in the case
   C. only if his detention is necessary for community production
   D. if commitment to a correctional institution had been under consideration before he was placed on probation

49. In dealing with violations of probation which have resulted in arrest, the probation officer should FIRST   49._____

   A. arrange for an immediate hearing before the sentencing judge in the original case
   B. discuss and evaluate the new violation with the arresting officer
   C. place a detainer against the probationer
   D. secure a voluntary statement from the probationer, including mention of his guilt or innocence

50. A probation officer sees a man on the street whom he believes is being sought under warrant as a probation violator. The probationer is not under his supervision. Of the following, the FIRST action the probation officer should take is to   50._____

   A. identify himself to the man and attempt to determine the latter's identity
   B. warn the probationer and report to his office that he has seen the violator
   C. advise the probationer to give himself up
   D. immediately contact the probation officer who has been supervising this probationer

---

KEY (CORRECT ANSWERS)

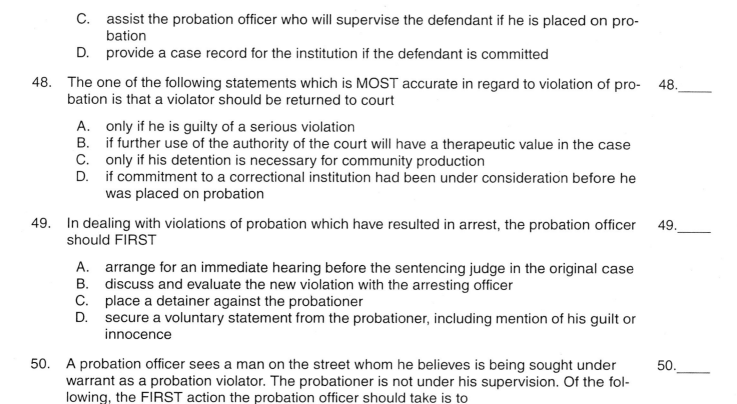

1. B	11. A	21. A	31. C	41. C
2. D	12. D	22. A	32. A	42. A
3. B	13. B	23. D	33. D	43. D
4. A	14. C	24. C	34. A	44. D
5. C	15. D	25. D	35. A	45. B
6. C	16. A	26. D	36. A	46. B
7. B	17. D	27. B	37. D	47. B
8. D	18. D	28. A	38. B	48. B
9. B	19. C	29. C	39. A	49. B
10. C	20. C	30. A	40. D	50. A

EXAMINATION SECTION
TEST 1

DIRECTIONS: Each question or incomplete statement is followed by several suggested answers or completions. Select the one that BEST answers the question or completes the statement. *PRINT THE LETTER OF THE CORRECT ANSWER IN THE SPACE AT THE RIGHT.*

1. One of the earliest of the names associated with the probation movement is   1.____

    A. Homer Folks   B. Ben Lindsey
    C. Helen D. Pigeon   D. John Augustus

2. Of the following, the fundamental theory of probation rests MOST NEARLY on   2.____

    A. the fear of punishment
    B. exercise by the court of its power of compulsion
    C. a promise by the offender to better his ways
    D. the frequency of recidivism

3. Release of offenders under supervision as an alternative to punishment was FIRST developed as a legal system in   3.____

    A. Ancient Rome   B. France
    C. the United States   D. Great Britain

4. The social agency conducting an institution for the care and treatment of delinquent and emotionally disturbed boys, which was founded originally for the care of Black children only, is the   4.____

    A. Wiltwyck School   B. Vanderbilt Clinic
    C. Craig Colony   D. Claremont House

5. A probation officer encountering a reference to *prognosis* in a case report would MOST accurately associate the term with   5.____

    A. a casual relationship   B. psychosis
    C. a congenital disease   D. a forecast

6. A probation report which describes a youngster as perspicacious seeks to convey the impression to the reader that the youngster is   6.____

    A. loquacious   B. clever
    C. shrewish   D. garrulous

7. In reporting on a person who thinks he sees objects which are NOT present and may NOT be real, the probation officer should describe such an individual as having   7.____

    A. claustrophobia   B. delusions
    C. hallucinations   D. paranoia

8. A good probation report should possess some of the following qualities, the LEAST desirable of which is   8.____

    A. legibility   B. clarity
    C. coherence   D. invalidity

9. When interviewing an individual with a reputation for being a conciliatory person, the pro-   9.____
bation officer should MOST reasonably expect to find that he

    A. is flippantly smooth
    B. has an appeasing manner
    C. is fickle
    D. has an uncontrollable temper

10. A juvenile whose veracity is frequently doubted is BEST described as   10.____

    A. a fabricator   B. an alien
    C. born out of wedlock   D. underprivileged

11. An adolescent who is habitually discontented could BEST be described as   11.____

    A. invidious   B. plaintive
    C. quibbling   D. captious

12. Siblings are MOST easily identified by   12.____

    A. blood   B. adoption proceedings
    C. color   D. speech

13. Occupational therapy is MOST closely associated with   13.____

    A. vocational guidance   B. position classification
    C. curative handicraft   D. diathermic treatment

14. Of the following degrees of deviation from normal mentality, the one indicating the   14.____
LEAST intelligence is the

    A. moron   B. imbecile
    C. idiot   D. borderline

15. The person whose duty it is to manage the estate of a minor or of an incompetent is   15.____
called the

    A. executor   B. probate officer
    C. amicus curiae   D. guardian

16. An order for a witness to appear in court is called   16.____

    A. a subpoena   B. an injunction
    C. a mandamus   D. res judicata

17. *Ostensibly a sane person, yet severely mentally ill and dangerous to himself and others*   17.____
is a description MOST commonly applied to a

    A. psychopath   B. paraplegic
    C. paretic   D. paranoid

18. The impact upon society of mental disease is MOST adequately indicated by   18.____

    A. its responsibility for sex crimes and delinquency
    B. the phenomenal growth of feeble-mindedness in the United States
    C. the increasing number of deaths resulting from it
    D. the burden of its disabling effects on the community

19. A deficiency disease is a disorder caused by a(n)   19.____

    A. deficiency of medical aid
    B. diet lacking certain vitamins or minerals
    C. lack of proper rest and relaxation
    D. insufficient quantity of sugar in the diet

20. Delinquency on the part of a child is believed to result PRIMARILY from   20.____

    A. emotional and personality maladjustments
    B. environmental handicaps
    C. physical disability
    D. sociological factors

21. In determining whether or not an offender should be placed on probation, the MOST   21.____
important factor for the probation officer to consider is the

    A. attitude of the community
    B. personality of the offender
    C. offense
    D. attitude of the court

22. A probation officer who has an objective attitude in social research would   22.____

    A. deal only with concrete reality rather than with abstract ideas
    B. use only evidence favorable to the objective
    C. object to all new hypotheses
    D. follow the evidence regardless of personal interests

23. In collecting social evidence from personnel in the public school system of the city, a pro-   23.____
bation officer would expect to find that the one of the following who makes the BEST
social witness is the

    A. principal of the school at which the offender was a pupil
    B. superintendent of schools
    C. teacher who is able to individualize his pupils
    D. truant officer

24. The BEST of the following reporting techniques in releasing statistical data of a social   24.____
nature is to publish

    A. percentage figures
    B. ratio figures
    C. absolute figures
    D. a descriptive summary without such figures

25. Progressively minded probation officers agree that the type of social treatment given a   25.____
delinquent should be determined PRIMARILY by the

    A. nature of the offense committed
    B. type and variety of social problems causing the delinquency
    C. size of the probation officer's case load
    D. plan recommended by the judge

26. From a psychological point of view, delinquency can MOST accurately be considered as   26.____
    A. a definite congenital trait which causes inability to adjust to society
    B. overt acts which come into conflict with natural instincts
    C. a symptom of a deeper maladjustment which manifests itself in an inability to adjust to society
    D. none of the above

27. The TRUE extent of delinquency and crime in the United States is   27.____
    A. known accurately on an annual basis
    B. estimated on an annual basis
    C. known accurately in certain fields
    D. gathered statistically during each census year

28. The belief that crime can be prevented BEST by enforcing laws rigidly is based on the theory that   28.____
    A. persons cannot continue criminal careers as freely during periods of incarceration
    B. suppression leads to sublimation
    C. punishment is the most effective deterrent known against lawbreakers
    D. multiplicity of laws causes confusion in their attempted enforcement

29. Studies of penology reveal that punishment has   29.____
    A. seldom served as a crime deterrent
    B. successfully served as a crime deterrent
    C. served as a crime deterrent only in cases of larceny
    D. not served as a crime deterrent because the penalties inflicted have been too moderate

30. In the classifications of crime listed below, the one in which the probation officer would expect to find the HIGHEST proportion of arrests of females would be recorded in uniform crime reports under the heading of   30.____
    A. assault   B. automobile theft
    C. burglary   D. rape

31. A national magazine conducting a long-term feature devoted to techniques of crime prevention regularly prints contributions from such persons as an ex-president of the United States, a mayor, a congressman, a governor, and a civil court judge.
    A probation officer would MOST logically conclude from this example that   31.____
    A. there is as yet a great deal of inconclusive thinking on the causes of crime and the treatment of those causes
    B. public officials are better judges of the effectiveness of crime prevention techniques than persons not in the public service
    C. the experiences of sociologists and psychiatrists have been wholly negative in the field of crime prevention
    D. the best approach to crime prevention is that which encompasses the activities of local, state, and federal officials of every type

32. The PRIMARY reason for recording the results of a probation investigation is that the   32._____

    A. law requires that this be done
    B. written record is more impressive and credible than an oral report
    C. reader exerts a minimum of effort in comprehending and digesting the information
    D. data obtained may be made secretly and permanently available

33. According to studies conducted on methods of questioning during intake procedure by   33._____
interviewers such as probation officers, a truthful statement of fact is LEAST easily
obtained from the person being questioned if he is

    A. allowed to use an uninterrupted narrative form of expression
    B. cross-examined frequently by the person doing the interviewing
    C. encouraged to present his facts in chronological order
    D. interrupted as seldom as possible

34. The CHIEF concern of the pre-sentence investigation in a criminal court should be,   34._____
according to the views expressed by the most noted researchers in the field of probation,
to

    A. speed up the court procedures so that more cases can be handled expeditiously
    B. discover the immediate cause of the offender's being brought before the court
    C. determine whether the person brought before the court is innocent or guilty of the
charges lodged against him
    D. explore all the social factors that have a bearing on the personality and behavior of
the offender

35. To a probation officer, the ultimate object of a pre-sentence investigation is   35._____

    A. knowledge that will insure the punishment of the offender if a crime has been com-
mitted
    B. knowledge that will protect society from the criminal
    C. understanding of the offender from the point of view of his possible re-integration
as a self-sufficient and permanently useful member of society
    D. understanding of the offender that will explain why he committed the crime and will
enable society to guard against that sort of criminal activity

36. Case study procedure differs from statistical procedure MOST markedly in that   36._____

    A. the basis for statistical study is observation
    B. statistical procedure can be divided into inventory, analysis, and inference
    C. incorrect data in statistical procedure may result in an incomplete analysis
    D. statistical procedure has a broad numerical base making restriction of subjects
necessary

37. Suppose that a good probation department were identified by each of the features listed   37._____
below.
If you, a probation officer, were studying the organization of such an agency, you would
expect to find its correctional program LEAST affected by the removal of its

    A. enlightened policies
    B. trained and competent personnel
    C. suitable equipment and supplies with which to have its work done
    D. advisory board of the most notable penologists in the country

38. The one of the following which BEST expresses one of the fundamental foundations of the probation system is a(n)

    A. desire to reward the first offender in order to encourage good conduct
    B. desire to protect society by facilitating the readjustment of the probationer
    C. economy measure designed to save the government the cost of supporting prisoners in institutions
    D. growing attitude of leniency toward offenders

38._____

39. From the point of view of the probation officer, to integrate into normal groups children presenting symptoms of mild behavior disorder would be

    A. too radical a proposal; it has never been tried successfully
    B. impracticable; participation of problem children would jeopardize the program of the other children in the group
    C. undesirable; children otherwise emotionally stable would tend to become corrupted
    D. beneficial; it would expose the problem children to the beneficent effect of group activity with children possessing conforming behavior patterns

39._____

40. The detention of children waiting for a court decision as to whether they should be retained on a charge of having committed a minor offense is considered socially undesirable by progressively minded probation officers because the

    A. children may be cleared of the charge and, therefore, found to have been detained without cause
    B. children may be subjected to emotional damage
    C. parents may become unnecessarily concerned over the children's absence from home
    D. community is charged with the expense of lodging and feeding the children

40._____

41. Of the PRIMARY functions of a modern police department in dealing with juvenile delinquency, one should be to

    A. arrest the parents of delinquents and hold them responsible for neglecting their duties as parents
    B. perform social case work with the families of delinquent children
    C. recommend the level of treatment for children presenting behavior problems
    D. take an active part in programs designed to prevent juvenile delinquency

41._____

42. Legally, the BEST definition of juvenile delinquency is: Any child under

    A. 18 who has deserted his home and who habitually associates with dissolute, vicious, or immoral persons
    B. 16 who has violated a city ordinance or who has committed any offense, except murder or manslaughter, against the laws of the state
    C. 18 who has violated a city ordinance or who has committed any offense, except murder or manslaughter, against the laws of the state
    D. 16 who is habitually disobedient to the reasonable and lawful commands of his parents and who habitually absents himself from school or who persistently violates school regulations

42._____

43. Current interest in child guidance clinics was developed because of an increasing belief that

    A. at least one-tenth of the nation's youth is destined to end in prison if not given systematic guidance
    B. children should be treated as miniature adults
    C. many of the emotional and mental disabilities of later life result from unfortunate childhood experiences
    D. the best interests of the nation require standardization of each child's education

43.____

44. A probationary sentence, such as the one given Joseph Buttafuoco for statutory rape of Amy Fisher, has its PRIMARY effect in

    A. punishing the defendant
    B. deterring such acts
    C. showing the public that justice has been meted out
    D. allowing a defendant to plead guilty and walk

44.____

45. During a period of probation in which records were kept for 360 children fourteen to eighteen years of age, probation officers found that the group committed certain offenses, as shown in the following table:

I.Q.	No. of Offenders	No. of Offenses	Offenses Per Offender
61-80	125	338	2.7
81-100	160	448	2.8
101 and over	75	217	2.9

According to the above data,
    A. the more intelligent offenders are no more law-abiding than, and perhaps not so law-abiding as, the dull offenders
    B. brighter offenders present no more difficult problems than less intelligent offenders
    C. the majority of this probation group is found to be above the average in intelligence of a normal group of young persons within this age range
    D. the relationship between the effectiveness of probation work and the number of offenders is in inverse ratio

45.____

46. The fundamental desires for food, shelter, family, and approval, and their accompanying instinctive forms of behavior, are among the most important forces in human life because they are essential to and directly connected with the preservation and the welfare of the individual as well as of the race.
According to this statement,

    A. as long as human beings are permitted to act instinctively, they will act wisely
    B. the instinct for self-preservation makes the individual consider his own welfare rather than that of others
    C. racial and individual welfare depend upon the fundamental desires
    D. the preservation of the race demands that instinctive behavior be modified

46.____

47. The growth of our cities, the increasing tendency to move from one part of the country to another, the existence of people of different cultures in the neighborhood, have together made it more and more difficult to secure group recreation as part of informal family and neighborhood life.
According to this statement,

47.____

A. the breaking up of family and neighborhood ties discourages new family and neighborhood group recreation
B. neighborhood recreation no longer forms a significant part of the larger community
C. the growth of cities crowds out the development of all recreational activities
D. the non-English speaking people do not accept new activities easily

48. Sublimation consists in directing some inner urge, arising from a lower psychological level, into some channel of interest on a higher psychological level. Pugnaciousness, for example, is directed into some athletic activity involving combat, such as football or boxing, where rules of fair play and the ethics of the game lift the destructive urge for combat into a constructive experience and offer opportunities for the development of character and personality.
According to this statement,

    48.___

A. the manner of self-expression may be directed into constructive activities
B. athletic activities such as football and boxing are destructive of character
C. all conscious behavior of high psychological levels indicates the process of sublimation
D. the rules of fair play are inconsistent with pugnaciousness

49. The interest and curiosity that a child shows in sex matters and activities should be regarded by the probation officer as

    49.___

A. a normal interest to be dealt with as one deals with interest in other subjects
B. something to be disregarded on the assumption that the child will forget about the problem
C. something to be satisfied by some mythical explanation until the child is old enough to be initiated into the mystery involved
D. something to be suppressed by threat of punishment

50. When a gang is brought before the court for stealing, the probation officer, in making his pre-probation investigation, should

    50.___

A. deal unofficially with the younger ones and officially with the older members of the gang
B. organize a group of businessmen to take an interest in the members of the gang
C. recommend that the ringleaders be committed to a child welfare institution and that the others be placed on probation
D. study each member of the gang and deal with him according to his individual situation

KEY (CORRECT ANSWERS)

1. D	11. B	21. B	31. A	41. D
2. C	12. A	22. D	32. A	42. B
3. C	13. C	23. C	33. B	43. C
4. A	14. C	24. B	34. D	44. C
5. D	15. D	25. B	35. C	45. A
6. B	16. A	26. C	36. D	46. C
7. C	17. A	27. B	37. D	47. A
8. D	18. D	28. B	38. B	48. A
9. B	19. B	29. C	39. D	49. A
10. A	20. A	30. A	40. B	50. D

TEST 2

DIRECTIONS: Each question or incomplete statement is followed by several suggested answers or completions. Select the one that BEST answers the question or completes the statement. *PRINT THE LETTER OF THE CORRECT ANSWER IN THE SPACE AT THE RIGHT.*

1. The one of the following statements which can MOST conceivably be characterized as true is:

    A. Generally speaking, the younger a person is, the less easily he can be influenced by suggestion.
    B. If a probation officer has sufficient technical knowledge of his duties, it is not necessary for him to exercise tact in dealing with criminal offenders.
    C. A probation officer should reject entirely hearsay evidence in making a social diagnosis of a case.
    D. One of the characteristics of adolescence is a feeling in the child that he is misunderstood.

1.____

2. The statement that those parental attitudes are good which offer emotional security to the child BEST expresses the notion that

    A. emotionally secure children do not have feelings of aggression
    B. children should not be held accountable for their actions
    C. parental attitudes are inadequate which do not give the child feelings of belonging and freedom for experience
    D. a family in which there is economic dependence cannot be good for the child

2.____

3. When advised of the need for medical treatment over an extended period of time in a locality some distance from home, the parents of a child with a cardiac ailment decide to send him to a home in another town.
The BEST home for the child in this town would be one

    A. in which there are already residing two foster children who require rest and quiet
    B. in which the family is on relief
    C. in which there are two active boys of the same age as this child
    D. with the bathroom and bedroom on the second floor

3.____

4. Rehabilitation of an offender who has presented serious problems can probably be effected BEST by the probation officer who

    A. believes that the behavior is caused by maladjustment and tries to meet the offender's needs accordingly
    B. is kind and just, but punishes the offender for every lapse of good conduct
    C. keeps the offender under constant observation, making him conscious of his behavior deviations
    D. overlooks minor transgressions and rewards the offender for good behavior

4.____

5. Making an adjustment upon release under probation or parole, as the case may be, is believed by court workers to be EASIER for the

    A. probationer because the delayed action awaiting his release from probation serves to keep him aware of the necessity of continuing his normal life patterns
    B. parolee because he is able to idealize the security of the penitentiary in his recent experience

5.____

    C.   probationer because he has not been removed from his normal surroundings
    D.   parolee because frequent visits by family members and close friends during his imprisonment served to provide periodic psychologically uplifting experiences

6.   In the granting of probation to a war veteran, the question of leniency on that account should   6.____

    A.   not enter because greater leniency to the veteran would give him an unfair advantage over the non-veteran facing the bar with equal guilt
    B.   enter because the veteran has made a universally acknowledged contribution to the protection of our society and deserves the protection of his own interests in return
    C.   not enter because other important considerations involved in the probation process are the protection of society and the furthering of the best interests of the individual
    D.   enter because the military experiences of the veteran may have contributed to his being more irresponsible mentally than the non-veteran

7.   During a certain five-year period, it is found that only 66.4 arrests for incest occurred yearly in the city.
On the basis of this information, the MOST obvious inference for a probation officer to make is that   7.____

    A.   the research material on which the data are based is definitely incomplete
    B.   apprehension for incest can be expected in about 66.4% of the cases in which this crime is committed
    C.   very few cases of incest were committed in the city during the stated period
    D.   most cases of incest did not become matters of official police information in the city during the stated period

Questions 8-10.

DIRECTIONS: Questions 8 through 10 are to be answered on the basis of the facts given in the following case history.

<u>Tom Jones</u> - Age 13, I.Q. III

    Boy is in 6th grade, school work poor, citizenship fair. He does not constitute a serious behavior problem in school but is often truant.
<u>Relatives</u>

    Mother, 33 years of age, divorced father of boy and later remarried. Stepfather and boy did not get along. Stepfather is now out of the home and his whereabouts unknown. Mother is employed in a beauty parlor, earning $255 a week. No other income in family. Woman's mother, age 70, keeps house and looks after boy and his younger sister. Grandmother has absolutely no control over boy.

    Sister is 9 years of age, a frail child, never strong, and because of this fact has been *spoiled*.

    Boy is undersized, thin, nervous, irritable, and emotional. He likes to read and reads well. Likes WILD WEST and adventure stories. Boy seems fond of his mother. Family lives in a very poor neighborhood.

The mother has an older sister, married, and living on a ranch in Canada. The couple are reported to be fairly well-to-do and have no children. Their ranch is located in a rather remote section. Boy's own father is remarried and living in Seattle. He has two children by his last marriage. Mother is weak and easygoing, passionately fond of both of her children, but inclined to scold them one minute and pet them the next.

Reason Before Court

Boy has been involved with a group of older boys in a series of petty thieveries. Was gone from home for two days at one time and when he returned, told a tale of being kidnapped, which was found later to be entirely imaginary.

8. According to the facts given in the preceding case history, the MOST applicable of the following interpretations for the probation officer to make is   8.__

    A. economic factors play a minor part in this case
    B. the boy's taste in reading may indicate a tendency toward instability
    C. removal of the family to a better neighborhood may solve this problem
    D. this is a case for the school authorities to handle because of the truancy involved

9. The conclusion among the following LEAST likely to be reached in a probation report on this case is   9.__

    A. the boy's love of adventure and excitement probably contributes to his behavior problem
    B. since the mother lacks stability of character, it would be best to take both children from her
    C. the kidnapping tale, later found to be false, would indicate little possibility of a serious mental defect in the boy
    D. the security of the aunt and uncle's home would be a determining factor in any plan to place the boy with them

10. The one of the following findings LEAST likely to be approved by an experienced probation officer is   10.__

    A. the boy can be placed and continued on probation beyond his eighteenth birthday
    B. placement in an *ungraded* class in school might greatly benefit this boy
    C. this family should be referred to a welfare agency in order that the family budget may be supplemented
    D. the greater affection bestowed on the little sister and the consequent jealousy of the boy is probably one of the causes of delinquency

11. The one of the following which is the LEAST valid reason for keeping probation case records is to   11.__

    A. maintain an accurate record of the activities of the probationers
    B. meet the legal requirement
    C. provide a record which may be used in appealing from a conviction
    D. provide for continuity of service to the probationer

12. A probation officer is a professional person who has specialized knowledge and skills in the area of casework in an authoritative setting.
    When the period of probation is ended, good probation practice suggests that

    12.____

    A. the probation officer cease to be interested in the probationer since the case is closed
    B. if there has been a good relationship between officer and probationer, contacts may be continued over a period of years
    C. the probation officer should remain the only person with whom the probationer can feel completely comfortable and confident
    D. the probation officer should maintain continued interest in the probationer so that case files can be built up which may be useful with other probationers

13. The one of the following which, in cases of juvenile delinquency, is NOT an advantage of probation over commitment to an institution is that probation

    13.____

    A. offers an individualized form of treatment
    B. is less expensive
    C. gives greater protection to the community
    D. leaves the offender in his normal home surroundings

14. In order to alleviate the heavy overcrowding of detention homes, a practice sometimes used in the case of a child awaiting a hearing is his confinement in his own home during the hours when he is not engaged in specific authorized pursuits such as attending school or working.
    The one of the following which is LEAST likely to be a serious problem in home detention is the

    14.____

    A. inability of probation officers or caseworkers to exercise adequate supervision over the child
    B. deprivation of the child from the companionship of children of his age
    C. possibility that the child's family cannot be depended upon to observe the conditions of detention
    D. continual feeling of shame and embarrassment the child may have when in the company of his siblings or friends

15. Of the following, the CHIEF factor which limits the use of the services of private social casework agencies by probation departments is

    15.____

    A. the belief by probation departments that the private agencies are unable to give constructive services to the probationers
    B. that the law prohibits use of such services in most types of cases
    C. the reluctance of probationers to accept voluntarily the services of these agencies
    D. the prohibitive cost of these services to the courts

16. Environmental manipulation as an approach to treatment is often required in probation supervision.
Of the following, the BEST illustration of this approach is a case where the probation officer

    A. adopts a positive rather than a negative attitude toward the client's future after his probation is over
    B. suggests physical changes in the probationer's life and makes referrals to various social agencies for assistance
    C. applies his knowledge of casework techniques in every aspect of probation super-vision
    D. cautiously makes use of authority in supervision

16.____

17. The disparity in the terms of sentences imposed by different judges in criminal courts for identical crimes has been a cause for serious concern.
Of the following, the GREATEST problem involved in the imposition of sentence is that

    A. the judges do not have any basis on which to impose a sentence other than their own judgment
    B. a serious crime may be punishable by a shorter sentence than a minor offense
    C. some judges will enjoy greater popularity than others
    D. the term of sentence a criminal receives is within the limits set for his crime, dependent on varying standards of the judges

17.____

18. In penal administration, *indeterminate sentence* means a

    A. sentence the length of which depends upon the behavior and improvement of the convicted person while in prison
    B. long prison sentence at hard labor
    C. sentence with a minimum and a maximum term determined by the judge within statutory limits
    D. sentence based on circumstantial evidence

18.____

19. An agency which provides casework help to parent applicants in deciding whether placement of their children is the solution to the family's problem, and in making referrals to community resources if placement is not indicated, is the

    A. Jewish Child Care Association
    B. Little Flower House
    C. Sheltering Arms Children Service
    D. Wiltwyck School

19.____

20. An agency providing casework service with psychiatric consultation and psychological testing for girls including unmarried mothers is the

    A. George Junior Republic
    B. Youth Consultation Service
    C. Goddard Neighborhood Center
    D. Girl's Club

20.____

21. Jurisdiction over cases involving the protection and treatment of persons under 16 years of age is vested in the _____ Court.

    A. Family   B. Juvenile   C. Supreme   D. County

21.____

22. The basic objective of the Judiciary Article of this state is to establish   22._____

    A. unification of all courts in the city, leaving the courts in the rest of the state unchanged in jurisdiction

    B. a unified court system for the entire state with appropriate jurisdictions in each district

    C. a separate court for each category of cases and a separate category of cases for each court

    D. a statewide court for all civil cases and a statewide court for all criminal cases

23. A caseworker in a city agency is planning to refer one of her clients to a private agency in   23._____
the community.
The one of the following which is of GREATEST importance in insuring that the transfer will actually take place is that the

    A. agency is located within the client's proper district

    B. client will cooperate in bringing about such a transfer

    C. caseworker will assure the client that transfer does not mean rejection by the former

    D. agency does not require a fee in excess of what the client can afford

24. The one of the following agencies which provides numerous services to children including recreation, vacation, convalescent care, foster care, and psychiatric service is the   24._____

    A. Child Development Center   B. Child Welfare League of America
    C. Children's Aid Society   D. U.S. Children's Bureau

25. Of the following institutions for the chronically ill, the one to which a physically handicapped child would be referred is   25._____

    A. Bird S. Coler Memorial Hospital   B. Beth Abraham Home
    C. Farm Colony   D. Josephine Baird Home

26. In planning for the vocational rehabilitation of a physically handicapped person, the use   26._____
of the sheltered workshop can be a very helpful resource.
Of the following, the client for whom such service would be MOST appropriate is the one who

    A. will need a constructive way to spend his time for an indefinite period

    B. because of advanced age, is unable to compete in the labor market

    C. needs a transitional experience between his medical care and undertaking a regular job

    D. has a handicap which permanently precludes any gainful employment

27. A group counseling service to parents focused on the understanding of child development and parent-child relations is available through   27._____

    A. Childville

    B. The Arthur Lehman Counseling Service

    C. The State Association for Mental Health

    D. The Child Study Association of America

28. A patient is being discharged from an institutional setting following an initial diagnosis and stabilizing treatment for a diabetic condition of which he had not been aware. His doctor recommends a diet and medication regime for the patient to follow at home, but the patient is uncertain about his ability to carry this out on his own.
A community resource that might be MOST helpful in such a situation is a

    A. visiting nurse service
    B. homemaker service
    C. neighborhood health center
    D. dietitian's service

28.___

29. Experience pragmatically suggests that dislocation from cultural roots and customs makes for tension, insecurity, and anxiety. This holds for the child as well as the adolescent, for the new immigrant as well as the second-generation citizen.
Of the following, the MOST important implication of the above statement is that

    A. anxiety, distress, and incapacity are always personal and can be understood best only through an understanding of the child's present cultural environment
    B. in order to resolve the conflicts caused by the displacement of a child from a home with one cultural background to one with another, it is essential that the child fully replace his old culture with the new one
    C. no treatment goal can be envisaged for a dislocated child which does not involve a value judgment which is itself culturally determined
    D. anxiety and distress result from a child's reaction to culturally oriented treatment goals

29.___

30. Accepting the fact that mentally gifted children represent superior heredity, the United States faces an important eugenic problem CHIEFLY because

    A. unless these mentally gifted children mature and reproduce more rapidly than the less intelligent children, the nation is heading for a lowering of the average intelligence of its people
    B. although the mentally gifted child always excels scholastically, he generally has less physical stamina than the normal child and tends to lower the nation's population physically
    C. the mentally subnormal are increasing more rapidly than the mentally gifted in America, thus affecting the overall level of achievement of the gifted child
    D. unless the mental level of the general population is raised to that of the gifted child, the mentally gifted will eventually usurp the reigns of government and dominate the mentally weaker

30.___

31. The form of psychiatric treatment which requires the LEAST amount of participation on the part of the patient is

    A. psychoanalysis   B. psychotherapy
    C. shock therapy   D. non-directive therapy

31.___

32. Tests administered by psychologists for the PRIMARY purpose of measuring intelligence are known as _____ tests.

    A. projective   B. validating
    C. psychometric   D. apperception

32.___

33. In recent years there have been some significant changes in the treatment of patients in state psychiatric hospitals.
    These changes are PRIMARILY caused by the use of

    A. electric shock therapy
    B. tranquilizing drugs
    C. steroids
    D. the open ward policy

    33.____

34. The psychological test which makes use of a set of 20 pictures, each depicting a dramatic scene is known as the

    A. GOODENOUGH TEST
    B. THEMATIC APPERCEPTION TEST
    C. MINNESOTA MULTIPHASIC PERSONALITY INVENTORY
    D. HEALY PICTURE COMPLETION TEST

    34.____

35. One of the MOST effective ways in which experimental psychologists have been able to study the effects on personality of heredity and environment has been through the study of

    A. primitive cultures
    B. identical twins
    C. mental defectives
    D. newborn infants

    35.____

36. In hospitals with psychiatric divisions, the psychiatric function is PREDOMINANTLY that of

    A. the training of personnel in all psychiatric disciplines
    B. protection of the community against potentially dangerous psychiatric patients
    C. research and study of psychiatric patients so that new knowledge and information can be made generally available
    D. short-term hospitalization designed to determine diagnosis and recommendations for treatment

    36.____

37. Predictions of human behavior on the basis of past behavior frequently are inaccurate because

    A. basic patterns of human behavior are in a continual state of flux
    B. human behavior is not susceptible to explanation of a scientific nature
    C. the underlying psychological mechanisms of behavior are not completely understood
    D. quantitative techniques for the measurement of stimuli and responses are unavailable

    37.____

38. Socio-cultural factors are being re-evaluated in casework practice as they influence both the worker and the client in their participation in the casework process.
    Of the following factors, the one which is currently being studied MOST widely is the

    A. social class of worker and client and its significance in casework
    B. difference in native intelligence which can be ascribed to racial origin of an individual
    C. cultural values affecting the areas in which an individual functions
    D. necessity in casework treatment of the client's membership in an organized religious group

    38.____

39. Deviant behavior is a sociological term used to describe behavior which is not in accord with generally accepted standards. This may include juvenile delinquency, adult criminality, mental or physical illness.
    Comparison of normal with deviant behavior is USEFUL because it

    A. makes it possible to establish watertight behavioral descriptions
    B. provides evidence of differential social behavior which distinguishes deviant from normal behavior
    C. indicates that deviant behavior is of no concern to caseworkers
    D. provides no evidence that social role is a determinant of behavior

39.____

40. Alcoholism may affect an individual client's ability to function as a spouse, parent, worker, and citizen. Your responsibility to a client with a history of alcoholism is to

    A. interpret to the client the causes of alcoholism as a disease syndrome
    B. work with the alcoholic's family to accept him as he is and to stop trying to reform him
    C. encourage the family of the alcoholic to accept treatment
    D. determine the origins of his particular drinking problem, establish a diagnosis, and work out a treatment plan for him

40.____

41. There is a trend to regard narcotic addiction as a form of illness for which the current methods of intervention have not been effective.
    Research on the combination of social, psychological, and physical causes of addiction would indicate that social workers should

    A. oppose hospitalization of addicts in institutions
    B. encourage the addict to live normally at home
    C. recognize that there is no successful treatment for addiction and act accordingly
    D. use the existing community facilities differentially for each addict

41.____

42. A study of social relationships among delinquent and non-delinquent youth has shown that

    A. delinquent youths generally conceal their true feelings and maintain furtive contacts
    B. delinquents are more impulsive and vivacious than law-abiding boys
    C. non-delinquent youths diminish their active social relationships in order to sublimate any anti-social impulses
    D. delinquent and non-delinquent youths exhibit similar characteristics of impulsiveness and vivaciousness

42.____

43. The one of the following which is the CHIEF danger of interpreting the delinquent behavior of a child in terms of morality alone when attempting to get at its causes is that

    A. this tends to overlook the likelihood that the causes of the child's actions are more than a negation of morality and involve varied symptoms of disturbance
    B. a child's moral outlook toward life and society is largely colored by that of his parents, thus encouraging parent-child conflicts
    C. too careful a consideration of the moral aspects of the offense and of the child's needs may often negate the demands of justice in a case
    D. standards of morality may be of no concern to the delinquent and he may not realize the seriousness of his offenses

43.____

44. In visiting a school attended by children of a *hard-core* family by your agency, it would generally be ADVISABLE to   44.____

    A. keep the school visit a secret from the family so as not to embarrass the children
    B. encourage the parents to obtain all necessary information themselves
    C. inform the family only if you have secured positive information from the school
    D. have the family fully accept the purpose of the visit beforehand

45. In the process of *reaching out* to service multi-problem families, often many initial appointments are made with adolescents before their parents have received much sustained treatment.
This practice is   45.____

    A. *undesirable;* adolescents are still subject to parental control and, therefore, the parents should be the focus of treatment
    B. *desirable;* juvenile delinquency is the chief cause of difficulty in multi-problem families
    C. *undesirable;* parental distrust of the worker is increased, thus negating the worker's efforts
    D. *desirable;* adolescents are individual clients and should be so treated

46. A 9-year-old boy is living at home with his remarried, widowed mother, his stepfather, and his 3-year-old half-sister. The boy is being neglected and often severely mistreated by his mother and stepfather. The stepfather resents the boy's presence in the home.
After failing to correct the situation by discussions with the boy's mother and stepfather, the caseworker should recommend for the boy's welfare   46.____

    A. foster home placement in order to prevent his further mistreatment while corrective educational therapy is used on the parents
    B. permanent separation of the boy from his family as the best means of preventing his continued exposure to the unsatisfactory pressures in the household
    C. placement of the boy outside the household and a stern warning to the parents that similar action will be taken on behalf of the younger child should the situation warrant it
    D. temporary placement of the boy with a foster family until such time as the stepfather is no longer in the household

47. A deserted woman and her 13-year-old son have been receiving public assistance. The woman is drunk most of the time, is known to be consorting with men at all hours, and has been unresponsive to casework treatment. The son has been involved in a few minor incidents which have brought him to the attention of the authorities.
The BEST action for the caseworker to take at this point in order to keep the son from becoming an outright delinquent is to recommend that   47.____

    A. the mother be arrested and jailed for contributing to the delinquency of a minor and the son be sent to a reformatory
    B. no action be taken against the mother because that will lower her status in the eyes of her son and will further weaken family controls
    C. the son be temporarily placed in a foster home and the mother given treatment for alcoholism
    D. the son be committed to a corrective school where his bad habits can be corrected, since the mother is apparently too sick to assume her responsibilities toward her son

48. A caseworker in a city agency is planning to refer one of her clients to a private agency in   48.___
the community.
The one of the following which is of GREATEST importance in insuring that the transfer will actually take place is that the

    A. agency is located within the client's proper district
    B. client will cooperate in bringing about such a transfer
    C. caseworker will assure the client that transfer does not mean rejection by the
       former
    D. agency does not require a fee in excess of what the client can afford

49. In treating juvenile delinquents, it has been found that there are some who make better   49.___
social adjustment through group treatment than through an individual casework
approach.
In selecting delinquent boys for group treatment, the one of the following which is the
MOST important consideration is that

    A. the boys to be treated in one group be friends or from the same community
    B. only boys who consent to group treatment be included in the group
    C. the ages of the boys included in the group vary as much as possible
    D. only boys who have not reacted to an individual casework approach be included in
       the group

50. Multi-problem families are generally characterized by various functional indicators.   50.___
Of the following, the family which is MOST likely to be a multi-problem family is one
which has

    A. unemployed adult family members
    B. parents with diagnosed character disorders
    C. children and parents with a series of difficulties in the community
    D. poor housekeeping standards

———————

KEY (CORRECT ANSWERS)

1.	D	11.	C	21.	A	31.	C	41.	D
2.	C	12.	B	22.	B	32.	C	42.	B
3.	A	13.	C	23.	B	33.	B	43.	A
4.	A	14.	B	24.	C	34.	B	44.	D
5.	C	15.	C	25.	A	35.	B	45.	C
6.	C	16.	B	26.	C	36.	D	46.	A
7.	D	17.	D	27.	D	37.	C	47.	C
8.	C	18.	C	28.	A	38.	C	48.	B
9.	B	19.	A	29.	C	39.	B	49.	B
10.	A	20.	B	30.	A	40.	D	50.	C

EXAMINATION SECTION
TEST 1

DIRECTIONS: Each question or incomplete statement is followed by several suggested answers or completions. Select the one that BEST answers the question or completes the statement. *PRINT THE LETTER OF THE CORRECT ANSWER IN THE SPACE AT THE RIGHT.*

1. The one of the following which is the BEST description of a properly objective investiga-   1.____
tor is one who

    A. is friendly and sensitive to the client's feelings, without becoming emotionally involved
    B. is distant and impersonal, remaining unaffected by what the client says
    C. lets personal emotions enter as far as the client's situation calls for them
    D. becomes emotionally involved with the client's situation but without showing this involvement

2. The one of the following which is MOST necessary for successfully interviewing a person   2.____
who belongs to a culture different from that of the investigator is for the investigator to

    A. have some appreciation of the other culture
    B. ignore those cultural differences which lead to bias
    C. stay away from sensitive, "touchy" issues
    D. assume the mannerisms of people in the other cultures

3. In fact-finding interviews, it is generally assumed that the smaller the number of inter-   3.____
viewees, the greater the increase of reliability with the addition of others. The PROPER number of interviewees needed to insure the accuracy of information obtained *generally* depends upon the

    A. educational level of those interviewed
    B. number of people who have the required information
    C. directness of the questions asked
    D. variability of the information received

4. The one of the following which is generally MOST likely to be accurately described in an   4.____
interview by an interviewee is

    A. the presence of a large painting in the investigator's office
    B. the number of people in the investigator's waiting room
    C. space relations
    D. duration of time

5. The one of the following which is *generally* the BEST course of action for an investigator   5.____
to take when interviewing a person who is reluctant to tell what he knows about a matter under investigation is to

    A. be curt and abrupt and threaten the person with the consequences of his withholding information
    B. be firm and severe and pressure the person into telling the needed information
    C. be patient and candid with the person being questioned about the investigation since doing otherwise is not ethical

D. give the person false information about the investigation so he will give the needed information without realizing its importance

6. It is often recommended that an investigator prepare in advance a list of questions or top-   6._____
ics to be covered in an interview. The MAIN reason for using such a check list is to

A. allow investigations to be assigned to less efficient investigators
B. eliminate a large amount of follow-up paper work
C. aid the investigator in remembering to cover all important topics
D. aid the investigator in maintaining an objective distance from the person inter-
viewed

7. Usually, the CHIEF advantage of a directive approach in an interview is that   7._____

A. the investigator maintains control over the course of the interview
B. the person interviewed is more likely to be put at ease
C. the person interviewed is generally left free to direct the interview
D. the investigator will not suggest answers to the person interviewed

8. Usually, the CHIEF advantage of a non-directive approach by an investigator in conduct-   8._____
ing an interview is that

A. the investigator generally conceals what he is looking for in the interview
B. the person interviewed is more likely to express his true feelings about the topic
under discussion
C. the person interviewed is more likely to follow an idea introduced by the investiga-
tor
D. the investigator can keep the discussion limited to topics he believes to be relevant

9. The one of the following which is generally the *least likely* to be accurate in a description   9._____
of an event given to an investigator is a statement about

A. the presence of an object
B. the number of people, when their number is small
C. locations of people
D. duration of time

10. Assume that you, an investigator, are conducting a character investigation. In an inter-   10._____
view, the one of the following character traits of the person being interviewed which can
USUALLY be determined with a *good* degree of reliability is

A. honesty   B. dependability
C. forcefulness   D. perseverance

11. As an investigator, you have been assigned the task of obtaining a family's social history.   11._____
The BEST place for you to interview members of the family while obtaining this social
history would *generally* be in

A. the family's home
B. your agency's general offices
C. the home of a friend of the family
D. your own private office

12. You, an investigator, are checking someone's work history. The way for you to get the   12.____
MOST reliable information from a previous employer is to

    A. send personal letters; the employer will respond to the personal attention
    B. send form letters; the employer will cooperate readily since little time or effort is
    asked of him
    C. arrange a personal interview; the employer may offer information he would not care
    to put in a letter or speak over the phone
    D. telephone; this method is as effective as a personal interview and is much more
    convenient

13. The effect that attestation, or the formal taking of an oath, has on witness testimony is to   13.____

    A. decrease accuracy, since a witness under oath is more nervous about what is said
    B. make little difference, since the witness is not too swayed by an oath
    C. increase accuracy, since a witness under oath feels more responsibility for what is
    said
    D. eliminate inaccuracy unless there is deliberate perjury on the part of the witness

14. If an investigator obtains testimony from persons in interviews by means of interrogation   14.____
or asking questions rather than by letting the person freely relate the testimony, what is
said will GENERALLY be

    A. greater in range and less accurate
    B. greater in range and more accurate
    C. about the same in range and less accurate
    D. about the same in range and more accurate

15. Experienced investigators have learned to phrase their questions carefully in order to   15.____
obtain the desired response. Of the following, the question which would *usually* elicit the
MOST accurate answer is:

    A. "How old are you?"
    B. "What is your income?"
    C. "How are you today?"
    D. "What is the date of your birth?"

16. The one of the following questions which would *generally* lead to the LEAST reliable   16.____
answer is

    A. "Did you see a wallet?"
    B. "Was the German Shepherd gray?"
    C. "Didn't you see the stop sign?"
    D. "Did you see the guard on duty?"

17. Some investigators may make a practice of observing details of the surroundings when   17.____
interviewing in someone's home or office. Such a practice is *generally* considered

    A. *undesirable,* mainly because such snooping is an unwarranted, unethical invasion
    of privacy
    B. *undesirable,* mainly because useful information is rarely, if ever, gained this way
    C. *desirable,* mainly because, useful insights into the character of the person inter-
    viewed may be gained

D. *desirable,* mainly because it is impossible to evaluate a person adequately without such observation of his environment

18. The one of the following questions which will MOST often lead to a reliable answer is: 18.____

    A. "Was his hair very dark?"
    B. "Wasn't there a clock on the wall?"
    C. "Was the automobile white or gray?"
    D. "Did you see a motorcycle?"

19. The one of the following which can MOST accurately be determined by an investigator by means of interviewing is 19.____

    A. a persons's intelligence
    B. factual information about an event
    C. a person's aptitude for a specific task
    D. a person's perceptions of his own abilities

20. The one of the following which is *most likely* to help a person being interviewed feel at ease is for the investigator to 20.____

    A. let him start the conversation
    B. give him an abundance of time
    C. be relaxed himself
    D. open the interview by telling a joke

21. If the interviewee is to perceive some goal for himself in the interview and thus be motivated to participate in it, it is important that he clearly understand some of the aspects of the interview. Of the following aspects, the one the interviewee needs LEAST to understand is 21.____

    A. the purpose of the interview
    B. the mechanics of interviewing
    C. the use made of the information he contributes
    D. what will be expected of him in the interview

22. As an investigator working on a project requiring inter-agency cooperation, you find that employees of an agency involved in the project are constantly making it difficult for you to obtain necessary information. Of the following, the BEST action for you to take FIRST is to 22.____

    A. discuss the problem with your supervisor
    B. speak with your counterpart in the other agency
    C. discuss the problem with the head of the uncooperative agency
    D. contact the head of your agency

23. The investigator is justified in misleading the interviewee only when, in the investigator's judgment, this is clearly required by the problem being investigated. Such practice is 23.____

    A. *necessary;* there are times when complete honesty will impede a successful investigation
    B. *unnecessary ;* such a tactic is unethical and should never be employed
    C. *necessary;* an investigator must be guided by success rather than ethical considerations in an investigation

D. *unnecessary;* it is clearly doubtful whether such a practice will help the investigator conclude the investigation successfully

24. Assume that, in investigating a case of possible welfare fraud, it becomes necessary to hold an interview in the client's home in order to observe family interaction and conditions. Upon arriving, the investigator finds that the client's living room is noisy and crowded, with neighbors present and children running in and out. Of the following, the BEST course of action for the investigator to take is to   24.____

   A. conduct the interview in the living room after telling the children to behave, and asking the neighbors to leave
   B. tell the client that it is impossible to conduct the interview in the apartment, and make an appointment for the next day in the investigator's office
   C. suggest that they move from the living room into the kitchen where there is a table on which he can write
   D. try his best to conduct the interview in the noisy and crowded living room

25. You, an investigator, are giving testimony in court about a matter you have investigated. An attorney is questioning you in an abrasive, badgering way, and, in an insulting manner, calls into doubt your ability as an investigator. You lose your temper and respond angrily, telling the attorney to stop harassing and insulting you. Of the following, the BEST description of such a response is that it is *generally*   25.____

   A. *appropriate;* as a witness in court, you do not have to take insults from anybody, including an attorney
   B. *inappropriate; losing your* temper will show that you are weak and cannot be trusted as an investigator
   C. *appropriate;* a judge and jury will usually respect someone who responds strongly to unjust provocation
   D. *inappropriate;* such conduct is unprofessional and may unfavorably impress a judge and jury

KEY (CORRECT ANSWERS)

1.	A		11.	A
2.	A		12.	C
3.	D		13.	C
4.	A		14.	A
5.	C		15.	D
6.	C		16.	B
7.	A		17.	C
8.	B		18.	D
9.	D		19.	D
10.	C		20.	C

21.	B
22.	A
23.	A
24.	C
25.	D

———

TEST 2

DIRECTIONS: Each question or incomplete statement is followed by several suggested answers or completions. Select the one that BEST answers the question or completes the statement. *PRINT THE LETTER OF THE CORRECT ANSWER IN THE SPACE AT THE RIGHT.*

1. The reliability of information obtained increases with the number of persons interviewed. The more the interviewees differ in their statements, the more persons it is necessary to interview to ascertain the true facts. According to this statement, the dependability of the information about an occurrence obtained from interviews is related to   1.____

    A. how many people are interviewed
    B. how soon after the occurrence an interview can be arranged
    C. the individual technique of the interviewer
    D. the interviewer's ability to detect differences in the statements of interviewees

2. An investigator interviews members of the public at his desk. The attitude of the public toward this department will probably be LEAST affected by this investigator's   2.____

    A. courtesy   B. efficiency
    C. height   D. neatness

3. The *one* of the following which is NOT effective in obtaining complete testimony from a witness during an interview is to   3.____

    A. ask questions in chronological order
    B. permit the witness to structure the interview
    C. make sure you fully understand the response to each question
    D. review questions to be asked beforehand

4. The person MOST likely to be a good interviewer is one who   4.____

    A. is able to outguess the person being interviewed
    B. tries to change the attitudes of the persons he interviews
    C. controls the interview by skillfully dominating the conversation
    D. is able to imagine himself in the position of the person being interviewed

5. When you are interviewing someone to obtain information, the BEST of the following reasons for you to repeat certain of his exact words is to   5.____

    A. *assure* him that appropriate action will be taken
    B. *encourage* him to elaborate on a point he has made
    C. *assure* him that you agree with his point of view
    D. *encourage* him to switch to another topic of discussion

6. You are interviewing a client who has just been assaulted. He has trouble collecting his thoughts and telling his story coherently. Which of the following represents the MOST effective method of questioning under these circumstances?   6.____

    A. Ask questions which structure the client's story chronologically into units, each with a beginning, middle and end.
    B. Ask several questions at a time to structure the interview.

    C.   Ask open-ended questions which allow the client to respond in a variety of ways.
    D.   Begin the interview with several detailed questions in order to focus the client's attention on the situation.

7.   You are conducting an initial interview with a witness who expresses reluctance, even hostility, to being questioned. You feel it would be helpful to take some notes during the interview.
In this situation, it would be BEST to

    A.   put off note-taking until a follow-up interview, and concentrate on establishing rapport with the witness
    B.   explain the necessity of note-taking, and proceed to take notes during the interview
    C.   make notes from memory after the witness has left
    D.   take notes, but as unobtrusively as possible

8.   You are interviewing the owner of a stolen car about facts relating to the robbery. After completing his statement, the car owner suddenly states that some of the details he has just related are not correct. You realize that this change might be significant.
Of the following, it would be BEST for you to

    A.   ask the owner what other details he may have given incorrectly
    B.   make a note of the discrepancy for discussion at a later date
    C.   repeat your questioning on the details that were misstated until you have covered that area completely
    D.   explain to the owner that because of his change of testimony, you will have to repeat the entire interview

9.   Assume that you have been asked to get all the pertinent information from an employee who claims that she witnessed a robbery.
Which of the following questions is *least likely* to influence the witness's response?

    A.   "Can you describe the robber's hair?"
    B.   "Did the robber have a lot of hair?"
    C.   "Was the robber's hair black or brown?"
    D.   "Was the robber's hair very dark?"

10.   In order to obtain an accurate statement from a person who has witnessed a crime, it is BEST to question the witness

    A.   as soon as possible after the crime was committed
    B.   after the witness has discussed the crime with other witnesses
    C.   after the witness has had sufficient time to reflect on events and formulate a logical statement
    D.   after the witness has been advised that he is obligated to tell the whole truth

11.   Assume that your superior assigns you to interview an individual who, he warns, seems to be hightly "introverted." You should be aware that, during an interview, such a person is likely to

    A.   hold views which are highly controversial in nature
    B.   be domineering and try to control the direction of the interview
    C.   resist answering personal questions regarding his background
    D.   give information which is largely fabricated

12. A young woman was stabbed in the hand in her home by her estranged boyfriend. Her   12.____
mother and two sisters were at home at the time.
Of the following, it would generally be BEST to interview the young woman in the presence of

    A. her mother *only*
    B. all members of her immediate family
    C. members of the family who actually observed the crime
    D. the official authorities

13. The one of the following statements concerning interviewing which is LEAST valid is that   13.____

    A. skill in interviewing can be improved by knowledge of the basic factors involving relations between people
    B. interviewing should become a routine and mechanical practice to the skilled and experienced interviewer
    C. genuine interest in people is essential for successful interviewing
    D. certain psychological traits characterize most people most of the time

14. The initial interview will normally be more of a problem to the interviewer than any subse-   14.____
quent interviews he may have with the same person because

    A. the interviewee is likely to be hostile
    B. there is too much to be accomplished'in one session
    C. he has less information about the client than he will have later
    D. some information may be forgotten when later making record of this first interview

15. Continuous taking of notes during an interview is generally   15.____

    A. *desirable* because no important facts will be forgotten
    B. *undesirable* because it gives the person being interviewed a clue to the importance of the information being obtained from him
    C. *desirable* because the interviewer cannot write as fast as the person being interviewed can speak
    D. *undesirable* because it may put the person being interviewed ill at ease

16. "Carefullyplanned interviews tend to impose restrictions which leave little room for spon-   16.____
taneity." A flaw in this critiscism of the planned interview is that it does NOT take into account that

    A. a planned interview obviates the need for spontaneity
    B. even the planned interview may be flexible
    C. not all planned interviews impose restrictions
    D. restrictions that result from planning are undesirable

17. Writing up the interview into a systematic report is BEST done   17.____

    A. in the presence of the subject, so that mistakes can be corrected immediately
    B. within a reasonably short time after the interview, so that nothing is forgotten
    C. no sooner than several days after the interview, so that the interviewer will have had plenty of time to think about it
    D. with the help of someone not present at the interview, so that an objective view can be obtained

18. While you are conducting an interview, the telephone on your desk rings. Of the following, it would be BEST for you to

    A. ask the interviewer at the next desk to answer your telephone and take the message for you
    B. excuse yourself, pick up the telephone, and tell the person on the other end you are busy and will call him back later
    C. ignore the ringing telephone and continue with the interview
    D. use another telephone to inform the operator not to put calls through to you while you are conducting an interview

18.____

19. An interviewee is at your desk, which is quite near to desks where other people work. He beckons you a little closer and starts to talk in a low voice as though he does not want anyone else to hear him. Under these circumstances, the BEST thing for you to do is to

    A. ask him to speak a little louder so that he can be heard
    B. cut the interview short and not get involved in his problems
    C. explain that people at other desks are not eavesdroppers
    D. listen carefully to what he says and give it consideration

19.____

20. Of the following, the BEST way for a person to develop competence as an interviewer is to

    A. attend lectures on interviewing techniques
    B. practice with employees on the job
    C. conduct interviews under the supervision of an experienced instructor
    D. attend a training course in counseling

20.____

21. During the course of an interview, it would be LEAST desirable for the investigator to

    A. correct immediately any grammatical errors made by an interviewee
    B. express himself in such a way as to be clearly understood
    C. restrict the interviewee to the subject of the interview
    D. make notes in a way that will not disturb the interviewee

21.____

22. Suppose that you are interviewing an eleven year old boy. The CHIEF point among the following for you to keep in mind is that a child, as compared with an adult, is generally

    A. more likely to attempt to conceal information
    B. a person of lower intelligence
    C. more garrulous
    D. more receptive to suggestive questions

22.____

23. In interviewing a person, "suggestive questions" should be avoided because, among the following,

    A. the answers to leading questions are not admissible in evidence
    B. an investigator must be fair and impartial
    C. the interrogation of a witness must be formulated according to his mentality
    D. they are less apt to lead to the truth

23.____

24. Among the following, it is generally desirable to interview a person outside his home or office because

24.____

A. the presence of relatives and friends may prevent him from speaking freely
B. a person's surroundings tend to color his testimony
C. the person will find less distraction outside his home or office
D. a person tends to dominate the interview when in familiar surroundings

25. For the interviewing process to be MOST successful, the interviewer should generally   25._____

A. remind the person being interviewed that false statements will constitute perjury and will be prosecuted as such
B. devise a single and unvarying pattern for all interviewing situations
C. let the individual being interviewed control the content of the interview but not its length
D. vary his interviewing approach as the situation requires it

---

KEY (CORRECT ANSWERS)

1.	A	11.	C
2.	C	12.	D
3.	B	13.	B
4.	D	14.	C
5.	B	15.	D
6.	A	16.	B
7.	B	17.	B
8.	C	18.	B
9.	A	19.	D
10.	A	20.	C

21.	A
22.	D
23.	D
24.	A
25.	D

LOGICAL REASONING

The reasoning test assesses how well applicants can read, understand, and apply critical thinking skills to factual situations. Before entering your job, you will receive training that requires reading, understanding, and applying a wealth of detailed, written materials. Although some information must be memorized, much of the information you will use must be learned through independent reasoning. The test is, therefore, designed to select trainees who will be able to handle the academic workload and who will subsequently be able to handle complex reasoning and decision-making situations on the job.

The Logical Reasoning Questions

These sample questions are similar to the questions you will find in actual tests in terms of difficulty and format. Some of the questions in the test will be harder and some will be easier than those shown here.

Some of the questions in this manual deal with topics related to general government business. However, all of the questions in the actual test will deal with topics related to the work performed in entry-level positions. *You should remember, however, that knowledge of job-specific subject matter is NOT required to answer correctly the questions in this manual or the questions in the actual test.*

The kind of reading these questions require you to do is different from ordinary reading in which you just follow the general meaning of a series of sentences or paragraphs to see what the writer is saying about the topic. Instead, it is the kind of reading you must do with complex material when you intend to take some action or draw some conclusion based on that material.

This test asks you to make logical conclusions based on facts given in various paragraphs, and answering requires careful reading and focused thought about exactly what is given and what **is not** given. Therefore, you should read each question and the answer choices for each question very carefully before choosing your answer. The information below will give you some suggestions about how to approach this part of the test and some information about how you can improve your reasoning skills.

About the Questions

Reading the Paragraph (The Beginning of the Question)

There may be facts in the paragraph that may not always be true everywhere. However, it is important for testing purposes that you **accept** every fact in the paragraph as given or true. Also remember that, in this part of the test, you are not being judged on your knowledge of facts, but rather on your ability to read and reason on the basis of the facts presented to you.

Example of a Paragraph:

Law enforcement agencies use scientific techniques to identify suspects or to establish guilt. One obvious application of such techniques is the examination of a crime scene. Some substances found at a crime scene yield valuable clues under microscopic examination. Clothing fibers, dirt particles, and even pollen grains may reveal important information to the careful investigator. Nothing can be overlooked because all substances found at a crime scene are potential sources of evidence.

Reading the Question Lead-in

Each paragraph is followed by a lead-in statement that asks you to complete a sentence by choosing one of several phrases (possible answers) labeled (A) to (E). The lead-in sentence may be either positive or negative, as shown in the examples below:

From the information given above, it can be validly concluded that,
or
From the information given above, it CANNOT be validly concluded that,

It is important to focus on the lead-in statement because if you skim over it, you may miss a "**NOT**" and answer that question incorrectly. Positive lead-in statements are followed by four false conclusions (set of possible answers) and one correct conclusion (the correct answer). Your task is to find the correct one. Negative lead-in statements, by contrast, give you four correct conclusions and only one false conclusion; the task in these types of questions is to determine the one conclusion that **cannot** be supported by the facts in the paragraph (the false conclusion). If you do not pay close attention to negative lead-in questions, you could jump to the conclusion that the first correct option you read must be the right answer. The lead-in statement may also limit the possible answers in some way. For example, a lead-in statement such as

"from the information given above, it can be validly concluded that, during a crime scene investigation"

means that there might be different answers based on other times and places, but for the purpose of the test question, only conditions during a crime scene investigation (as described in the lead-in) should be considered.

The lead-in statement is followed by the set of conclusions or possible alternatives from which you will choose the correct answer. There are always five alternatives, which appear as follows:

A) all substances that yield valuable clues under microscopic examination are substances found at a crime scene
B) some potential sources of evidence are substances that yield valuable clues under microscopic examination
C) some substances found at a crime scene are not potential sources of evidence
D) no potential sources of evidence are substances found at a crime scene
E) some substances that yield valuable clues under microscopic examination are not substances found at a crime scene

Reasoning About Categories

Sometimes the information that you work with is based on your knowledge of how things can be categorized or grouped and combined with your knowledge of facts about those categories. You may have information about several categories that can be combined in various ways. You can also draw conclusions from facts that are not true and from facts about different events or indicators that are linked together. To understand these statements better, consider the following situation:

Think of a situation in which you are in charge of searching a vacant building for a missing child. The building has six floors. You have assigned one group to begin searching on the first floor of the building and then to move up to the next higher floor as they complete their search. A second group is sent to the top floor to begin searching there and then to move down as they complete searching. The first two floors of the building once contained a retail store and, therefore, broken glass shelves and metal hooks litter those floors. The next three floors once contained offices and, although they do not have any metal or broken glass on the floors, these floors do have plenty of leftover paper trash everywhere. The top floor used to be a penthouse apartment, and it is the only floor in the building that is still carpeted.

This situation gives you six floors that have in the past been used for three different purposes. There are two groups of searchers with two different search patterns. Within this situation, there are various categories into which information can be sorted. As the searchers report back to you on their progress, your level of certainty will depend on the completeness of the information you receive from them.

For example, if one group leader reports back "We've just finished searching a floor that is carpeted, and the child is not here," you **can** conclude that the child is not on the penthouse apartment level of the building. However, if the other group leader calls to say "We've just finished searching a floor with a lot of glass debris all over the place," you **cannot** conclude that the retail part of the building has been completely searched because the leader only told you about one floor while there were two floors in that category (two floors with glass all over the floor). However, if the leader told you "We've just finished searching two floors full of glass and metal hooks, and we're moving on to search the next floor up, where there seems to be a lot of paper all over," then you **could** conclude that the entire retail section had been searched because you have information that is complete about that category.

As you study the logical reasoning test questions, you must use the type of approach described above to reason about categories of information and draw conclusions through the process of elimination.

Statements Using the Quantifier "All"

One of the biggest mistakes people make when they jump to conclusions without basing them on all the facts is to misinterpret statements beginning with "all." A sentence that begins with the words "all" or "every" gives you information about how two different groups are linked. If a librarian told you "All the books on this set of shelves are about law enforcement," you might be tempted to conclude that all of the library's books on law enforcement were on that set of shelves, but you would be wrong. That sentence simply tells you that the books on those shelves are a subcategory of the category of books on law enforcement. That sentence does **not** tell you anything about where other law enforcement books are located in the library. Therefore, you do not have any information on the rest of that category.

It is easier to recognize the error in this kind of thinking if you consider two linked groups of things that are of very different sizes. Suppose a neighbor describes a children's birthday party at his house, saying "all the children at the party spoke Spanish fluently." It would not be correct to conclude that "all people who could speak Spanish fluently attended this birthday party." In this case, it is easy to recognize that "all the children at the party who spoke Spanish fluently" is really a subgroup of the category of "all people who could speak Spanish."

Reasoning From Disproved Facts ("NONE" and "NOT" Statements)

A lot of useful information can be gained when you learn that something is **NOT** true or when you know that one group of things is **NOT** part of a particular category. This is the same as saying that there is no overlap at all between two groups of things. Here, you can draw conclusions about either group as it relates to the other since you can count on the fact that the two groups have no members in common. If you can say "no reptiles are warm-blooded," you can also say "no warm-blooded creatures are reptiles" because you know that the first statement means that there is no overlap between the two categories. Many investigations hinge on negative facts. In the logical reasoning test part, you will see phrases such as "It is not the case that" or "Not all of the" or many words that begin with the prefix "non-." All of these are ways to say that a negative fact has been established.

Sometimes our ordinary speech habits get in the way. Most people would not make a statement such as "Some of the pizza has no pepperoni" unless they are trying to suggest at the same time that some of the pizza does have pepperoni. By contrast, a detective might make a statement such as "some of the bloodstains were not human blood" simply because only part of the samples had come back from the laboratory. The rest of the bloodstains might or might not be human.

As you work through the sample questions and practice test in this manual, think about each negative phrase or term you find. Take care to assume only as much as is definitely indicated by the facts as given, **AND NO MORE.**

READING COMPREHENSION
UNDERSTANDING AND INTERPRETING WRITTEN MATERIAL

EXAMINATION SECTION
TEST 1

DIRECTIONS: Each question or incomplete statement is followed by several suggested answers or completions. Select the one that BEST answers the question or completes the statement. *PRINT THE LETTER OF THE CORRECT ANSWER IN THE SPACE AT THE RIGHT.*

Questions 1-3.

DIRECTIONS: Questions 1 through 3 are to be answered SOLELY on the basis of the following passage.

The basic disparity between punitive and correctional crime control should be noted. The first explicitly or implicitly assumes the availability of choice or freedom of the will and asserts the responsibility of the individual for what he does. Thus the concept of punishment has both a moral and practical justification. However, correctional crime control, though also deterministic in outlook, either explicitly or implicitly considers criminal behavior as the result of conditions and factors present in the individual or his environment; it does not think in terms of free choices available to the individual and his resultant responsibility, but rather in terms of the removal of the criminogenic conditions for which the individual may not be responsible and over which he may not have any control. Some efforts have been made to achieve a theoretical reconciliation of these two rather diametrically opposed approaches but this has not been accomplished, and their coexistence in practice remains an unresolved contradiction.

1. According to the *correctional* view of crime control mentioned in the above passage, criminal behavior is the result of

    A. environmental factors for which individuals should be held responsible
    B. harmful environmental factors which should be eliminated
    C. an individual"s choice for which he should be held responsible and punished
    D. an individual's choice and can be corrected in a therapeutic environment

1._____

2. According to the above passage, the one of the following which is a problem in correctional practice is

    A. identifying emotionally disturbed individuals
    B. determining effective punishment for criminal behavior
    C. reconciling the punitive and correctional views of crime control
    D. assuming that a criminal is the product of his environment and has no free will

2._____

3. According to the above passage, the one of the following which is an ASSUMPTION underlying the punitive crime control viewpoint rather than the correctional viewpoint is that crime is caused by

    A. inherited personality traits
    B. poor socio-economic background
    C. lack of parental guidance
    D. irresponsibility on the part of the individual

3._____

Questions 4-9.

DIRECTIONS: Questions 4 through 9 are to be answered SOLELY on the basis of the following passage.

Man's historical approach to criminals can be conveniently summarized as a succession
of three R's: Revenge, Restraint, and Reformation. Revenge was the primary response prior
to the first revolution in penology in the 18th and 19th centuries. It was replaced during that
revolution by an emphasis upon restraint. When the second revolution occurred in the late
19th and 20th centuries, reformation became an important objective. Attention was focused
upon the mental and emotional makeup of the offender and efforts were made to alter these
as the primary sources of difficulty.

We have now entered yet another revolution in which a fourth concept has been added to
the list of R's: Reintegration. This has come about because students of corrections feel that a
singular focus upon reforming the offender is inadequate. Successful rehabilitation is a two-
sided coin, including reformation on one side and reintegration on the other.

It can be argued that the third revolution is premature. Society itself is still very ambivalent about the offender. It has never really replaced all vestiges of revenge or restraint, simply
supplemented them. Thus, while it is unwilling to kill or lock up all offenders permanently, it is
also unwilling to give full support to the search for alternatives.

4. According to the above passage, revolutions against accepted treatment of criminals   4.___
   have resulted in all of the following approaches to handling criminals EXCEPT

   A. revenge   B. restraint
   C. reformation   D. reintegration

5. According to the above passage, society NOW views the offender with   5.___

   A. uncertainty   B. hatred
   C. sympathy   D. acceptance

6. According to the above passage, the second revolution directed PARTICULAR attention   6.___
   to

   A. preparing the offender for his return to society
   B. making the pain of punishment exceed the pleasure of crime
   C. exploring the inner feelings of the offender
   D. restraining the offender from continuing his life of crime

7. According to the above passage, students of corrections feel that the lack of success of   7.___
   rehabilitation programs is due to

   A. the mental and emotional makeup of the offender
   B. vestiges of revenge and restraint which linger in correction programs
   C. failure to achieve reintegration together with reformation
   D. premature planning of the third revolution

8. The above passage suggests that the latest revolution will

    A. fail and the cycle will begin again with revenge or restraint
    B. be the last revolution
    C. not work unless correctional goals can be defined
    D. succumb to political and economic pressures

8.____

9. The one of the following titles which BEST expresses the main idea of the above passage is

    A. IS CRIMINAL JUSTICE ENOUGH?
    B. APPROACHES IN THE TREATMENT OF THE CRIMINAL OFFENDER
    C. THE THREE R'S IN CRIMINAL REFORMATION
    D. MENTAL DISEASE FACTORS IN THE CRIMINAL CORRECTION SYSTEM

9.____

Questions 10-15.

DIRECTIONS: Questions 10 through 15. are to be answered SOLELY on the basis of the following passage.

In a study by J.E. Cowden, an attempt was made to determine which variables would best predict institutional adjustment and recidivism in recently committed delinquent boys. The results suggested in particular that older boys, when first institutionalized, who are initially rated as being more mature and more amenable to change, will most likely adjust better than the average boy adjusts to the institution. Prediction of institutional adjustment was rendered slightly more accurate by using the variables of age and personality prognosis in combined form.

With reference to the prediction of recidivism, boys who committed more serious offenses showed less recidivism than average. These boys were also older than average when first committed. The variable of age accounts in part for both their more serious offenses and for their lower subsequent rate of recidivism.

The results also showed some trends suggesting that boys from higher socioeconomic backgrounds tended to commit more serious offenses leading to their institutionalization as delinquents. However, neither the ratings of socioeconomic status nor *home-environment* appeared to be significantly related to recidivism in this study.

Cowden also found an essentially linear relationship between personality prognosis and recidivism, and between institutional adjustment and recidivism. When these variables were used jointly to predict recidivism, accuracy of prediction was increased only slightly, but in general the ability to predict recidivism fell far below the ability to predict institutional adjustment.

10. According to the above passage, which one of the following was NOT found to be a significant factor in predicting recidivism?

    A. Age
    B. Personality
    C. Socioeconomic background
    D. Institutional adjustment

10.____

11. According to the above passage, institutional adjustment was MORE accurately pre-dicted when the variables used were

    A. socioeconomic background and recidivism
    B. recidivism and personality
    C. personality and age
    D. age and socioeconomic background

11.____

12. According to the above passage, which of the following were variables in predicting both recidivism and institutional adjustment?

    A. Age and personality
    B. Family background and age
    C. Nature of offense and age
    D. Personality

12.____

13. Which one of the following conclusions is MOST justified by the above passage?

    A. Institutional adjustment had a lower level of predictability and recidivism.
    B. Recidivism and seriousness of offense are negatively correlated to some degree.
    C. Institutional adjustment and personality prognosis, when considered together, are significantly better predictors of recidivism than either one alone.
    D. A delinquent boy from a lower class family background is more likely to have committed a serious first offense than a delinquent boy from a higher socio-economic background.

13.____

14. The study discussed in the above passage found that delinquent boys from a higher socioeconomic background tended to

    A. commit more serious crimes
    B. commit less serious crimes
    C. show more recidivism than average
    D. show less recidivism than average

14.____

15. The MOST appropriate conclusion to be drawn from the study discussed above is that

    A. delinquent boys from higher socioeconomic backgrounds show less institutional adjustment than average
    B. a high positive correlation was found between recidivism and institutional adjustment
    C. home environment, although not significantly related to recidivism, did influence institutional adjustment
    D. older boys are more likely to commit more serious first offenses and show less recidivism than younger boys

15.____

Questions 16-18

DIRECTIONS: Questions 16 through 18 are to be answered SOLELY on the basis of the fol-lowing passage.

Educational programming of the offender has become part of the dominant philosophy in the correctional community. Due to the recent increase in national funding for demonstration prison education projects, future research endeavors may well be facilitated so that we can better evaluate the effectiveness of specific educational approaches. Research on past programs has resulted in various conclusions as to their effectiveness in the reduction of recidivism. Even though some programs have seemed promising, when they are properly evaluated, the initial results have been found to be spurious. Invalidity stemmed, by and large, from the fact that inmates shown to be *successful* in such educational programs may have *had it made* anyway, particularly when those selected for the program were the best risks. Success of the program was judged on the basis of a study of recidivism which, due to lack of funds, was of insufficient duration.

Research is the bookkeeping of corrections. Unfortunately, many correctional enterprises operate without such bookkeeping. When this happens, like businesses without bookkeeping, they may soon be bankrupt. However, unlike business, corrections can provide a steady salary for its employees even when it is bankrupt.

Despite these sad conclusions, effective program implementation can become a reality through continued experimentation and evaluation, utilizing acceptable methodological procedures and specially trained personnel, as well as having the necessary total institutional support.

16. According to the above passage, the apparent success of past correctional educational programs was due in LARGE part to   16.____

    A.   biased samples   B.   competent trainers
    C.   societal acceptance   D.   inferior goals

17. The second paragraph in the above passage states that *Research is the bookkeeping of corrections.*   17.____
Which of the following MOST accurately describes what is meant by this statement?

    A.   Since correctional facilities are government institutions, only records of government research grants and the use of those grants can indicate when the institution is in financial difficulty.
    B.   Research provides to correctional institutions information which is essential for their decision-making process.
    C.   Without grants for research, correctional institutions will become financially bankrupt even though they are still able to pay employee salaries.
    D.   Correctional institutions must keep abreast of research or they will find themselves educationally bankrupt.

18. According to the above passage, the future of educational programming is brighter than its past because of   18.____

    A.   social awareness
    B.   longer programs
    C.   increased national funding
    D.   more highly qualified administrators

Questions 19-23.

DIRECTIONS: Questions 19 through 23 are to be answered SOLELY on the basis of the following passage.

The social problems created by the urban delinquent gang member require the attention and resources of the entire community. Recent studies have shown that we are dealing with a boy who early in life has his first official contact with the police and who, shortly afterwards, is bound for juvenile court. The gang member commits several delinquencies before reaching adult status and the earlier his onset of delinquency, the more serious become his violations of the law. There is also evidence of increasingly serious delinquency involvement of a substantial proportion of the gang members. Of major significance are the shorter periods of time between each succeeding offense and the delinquents' employment or threat to employ force and violence.

All of these findings testify to the urgent need for prevention and treatment to be directed at pre- and early adolescence and to be sensitive to the importance of the first signs of youthful disregard for society's legal norms. Follow-up studies on delinquent gang members revealed that forty percent of the gang members continued into adult crime. For several reasons, this is a minimal figure and should probably be twenty percent higher. It is reasonable to infer that, given more thorough follow-up techniques and a longer follow-up period, an appreciable number of those for whom no criminal records were located will acquire them. In any event, these studies have revealed a strong linkage between delinquency and crime. This linkage has been established by following up a group of gang members into adulthood rather than by tracing back a group of adult offenders into delinquency, and by utilizing a sample of juveniles dealt with by the police rather than those appearing before a juvenile court, or in a clinic.

19. According to the above passage, as delinquents get older, their crimes GENERALLY become _____ serious _____ frequent.   19._____

    A. more; and more   B. more; but less
    C. less; but more   D. less; and less

20. The above passage SUGGESTS that delinquents should receive   20._____

    A. severe punishment at the time of their first offense
    B. institutional care until such time that they may prove themselves capable of functioning in a free society
    C. treatment at pre- and early adolescence at the first signs of disregard for societal norms
    D. continuous psychological counseling from the time of their first offense until the delinquent reaches legal age

21. According to the above passage, delinquent gang members pose a problem which should be the responsibility of the   21._____

    A. community   B. police
    C. courts   D. social worker

22. According to the above passage, follow-up studies on delinquent gang members have underestimated the percent of gang members who continued to adult crime because   22._____

    A. their sample was biased as it only involved urban gang members
    B. the studies did not follow the *career* of the sample group for a long enough period of time
    C. the studies concerned only those juveniles who, as adults, were dealt with by the police and not those who appeared in court or were referred to a clinic

D. the method used, that of following up a group of gang members rather than tracing back a group of adult offenders, was invalid

23. According to the above passage, the ACTUAL percent of delinquent gang members who continue into adult crime is MOST NEARLY

23.____

A. 20% B. 40% C. 50% D. 60%

Questions 24-25.

DIRECTIONS: Questions 24 and 25 are to be answered SOLELY on the basis of the following passage.

The criminal justice system is generally regarded as having the basic objective of reducing crime. However, one must also consider its larger objective of minimizing the total social costs associated with crime and crime control. Both of these components are complex and difficult to measure completely. The social costs associated with crime come from the long- and short-term physical damage, psychological harm, and property losses to victims as a result of crimes committed. Crime also creates serious indirect effects. It can induce a feeling of insecurity that is only partially reflected in business losses and economic disruption due to anxiety about venturing into high crime rate areas.

Balanced against these costs associated with crime must be the consequences of actions taken to reduce them. Money spent on developing, maintaining, and operating criminal justice agencies is part of the cost of the crime control system. But there are also indirect costs, such as welfare payments to prisoners' families, income lost by offenders who are denied good jobs, legal fees, and wages lost by witnesses. In addition, there are penalties suffered by suspects erroneously arrested or sentenced, the limitation on personal liberty resulting from police surveillance, and the invasion of privacy in maintaining criminal records.

24. According to the above passage, all of the following are indirect costs of the crime control system EXCEPT

24.____

A. wages lost by witnesses
B. money spent for legal services
C. payments made to the families of prisoners
D. money spent on operating criminal justice agencies

25. According to the above passage, actions taken to reduce crime

25.____

A. will reduce the indirect costs of the crime control system
B. may result in a decrease of personal liberty
C. may cause psychological harm to victims of crime
D. should immediately start improving the criminal justice system

KEY (CORRECT ANSWERS)

1.	B		11.	C
2.	C		12.	A
3.	D		13.	B
4.	A		14.	A
5.	A		15.	D
6.	C		16.	A
7.	C		17.	B
8.	C		18.	C
9.	B		19.	A
10.	C		20.	C

21.	A
22.	B
23.	D
24.	D
25.	B

TEST 2

DIRECTIONS: Each question or incomplete statement is followed by several suggested answers or completions. Select the one that BEST answers the question or completes the statement. *PRINT THE LETTER OF THE CORRECT ANSWER IN THE SPACE AT THE RIGHT.*

Questions 1-4.

DIRECTIONS: Questions 1 through 4 are to be answered SOLELY on the basis of the following passage.

The initial contact between the offender and the correctional social worker frequently occurs at the point of extreme crisis, when the usual adaptive mechanisms have been broken down. In many areas of correctional practice, such as probation and parole, this contact is often followed by long periods during which limited freedom is officially imposed. It is at such points that response to the offer of hope for restoring equilibrium may mean most, and that new coping capacities and new person-environment relationships develop. As a result, many correctional social workers have become skilled in strategies of crisis intervention. What they learn from such endeavors does not generally find its way into the professional literature; thus, the correctional social worker has contributed little to developing and testing practice theory. However, beginning efforts are being made to remedy this situation, and it is probable that corrections may provide an important laboratory from which tomorrow's understanding of the theory and strategies of crisis intervention will emerge.

1. Which of the following is the MOST appropriate title for the above passage?   1.____

    A. CORRECTIONAL SOCIAL WORK IN CRISIS
    B. CRISIS INTERVENTION AND CORRECTIONAL SOCIAL WORK
    C. COPING CAPACITIES OF PROBATIONERS AND PAROLEES
    D. THE THEORY AND PRACTICE OF CRISIS INTERVENTION

2. It can be concluded from the above passage that crisis intervention as a method of treatment and rehabilitation in correctional social work is based on the premise that a(n)   2.____

    A. offender may be more likely to respond to help and change his life style at a time of crisis, such as being on probation or parole, when incarceration is the only other alternative
    B. person is not likely to respond to help and change his life style unless he is in a crisis situation, such as being on probation or parole, when he is threatened by imprisonment
    C. offender sentenced to probation or parole is likely to respond to help and change his life style, because his freedom is limited and supervision is imposed on him
    D. situation such as probation or parole, in which an offender is supervised and his freedom is limited, presents ideal conditions for constructive personality change

3. On the basis of the above passage, it would be VALID to assume that   3.____

    A. offenders sentenced to probation and parole usually develop coping capacities which would not emerge during imprisonment
    B. offenders who are rehabilitated as a result of probation and parole have greater coping capacities in crisis situations

    C.   a life crisis situation such as being sentenced to probation or parole may become a positive force toward an offender's rehabilitation

    D.   an offender's ability to develop new coping capacities in times of crisis should be a decisive factor in determining the recommended sentence

4.   According to the above passage, correctional social workers' experiences in crisis inter-   4._____
vention have

    A.   encouraged use of crisis intervention strategy
    B.   contributed to theory rather than practice
    C.   not resulted in further learning
    D.   not generally been reported in print

Questions 5-9.

DIRECTIONS: Questions 5 through 9 are to be answered SOLELY on the basis of the following passage.

    The group worker must be concerned with two major goals in correctional treatment of juvenile offenders: (a) sustaining and reinforcing conventional value systems, and (b) enhanc-ing the youth's positive self image and general feeling of worthiness. The group processes involved in working toward these ends are so interrelated that treatment can meet both goals by improving interpersonal skills and experiences. As an initial concept, it is important to recognize that, in spite of delinquent behavior, adolescents usually do exhibit conscience for-mation, as may be seen in their support of conformity values, evidence of guilt and conven-tional behavior, and rationalization of delinquent behavior. It is this very ambivalence toward the conventional order that can be the basis for rehabilitation. On the basis of the distinction between real guilt and guilt reflecting emotional problems, an ideal therapeutic objective is to reach the point at which the internal and external controls are in general harmony and agency expectations are closely allied to and consistent with group and individual expectations.

5.   Which of the following is the BEST title for the above passage?   5._____

    A.   GROUP TREATMENT OF JUVENILE OFFENDERS
    B.   THE GROUP WORKER AND CORRECTIONAL TREATMENT
    C.   THE JUVENILE OFFENDER
    D.   CONSCIENCE FORMATION IN JUVENILE OFFENDERS

6.   On the basis of the above passage, it would be VALID to assume that group treatment of   6._____
the juvenile offender can result in the development of

    A.   greater self-confidence
    B.   rationalization of delinquent behavior
    C.   guilt and conscience formation
    D.   increased conscientiousness

7.   On the basis of the above statement, it would be VALID to conclude that juvenile offend-   7._____
ers

    A.   are anxious for rehabilitation
    B.   have no internal or external controls
    C.   are deficient in interpersonal skills and experiences

D. feel more guilt because of emotional problems than because of offenses committed

8. According to the above passage, a characteristic of juvenile offenders which makes them   8._____
amenable to correctional treatment is that they

A. can be reached by group processes
B. have a general feeling of worthiness
C. show signs of conscience formation
D. are ambivalent toward rehabilitation

9. According to the above passage, an IDEAL therapeutic objective in the group treatment   9._____
of juvenile offenders would be based on

A. agency expectations
B. group expectations
C. the distinction between real guilt and irrational guilt
D. the harmony between external and internal controls

Questions 10-14.

DIRECTIONS: Questions 10 through 14 are to be answered on the basis of the following passage.

Mental disorders are found in a fairly large number of the inmates in correctional institutions. There are no exact figures as to the number of inmates who are mentally disturbed -
partly because it is hard to draw a precise line between *mental disturbance* and *normality* -
but experts find that somewhere between 15% and 25% of inmates are suffering from disorders that are obvious enough to show up in routine psychiatric examinations. Society has not
yet really come to grips with the problem of what to do with mentally disturbed offenders.
There is not enough money available to set up treatment programs for all the people identified
as mentally disturbed; and there would probably not be enough qualified psychiatric personnel available to run such programs even if they could be set up. Most mentally disturbed
offenders are, therefore, left to serve out their time in correctional institutions, and the burden
of dealing with them falls on correction officers. This means that a correction officer must be
sensitive enough to human behavior to know when he is dealing with a person who is not
mentally normal, and that the officer must be imaginative enough to be able to sense how an
abnormal individual might react under certain circumstances.

10. According to the above passage, mentally disturbed inmates in correctional institutions   10._____

A. are usually transferred to mental hospitals when their condition is noticed
B. cannot be told from other inmates because tests cannot distinguish between
insane people and normal people
C. may constitute as much as 25% of the total inmate population
D. should be regarded as no different from all the other inmates

11. The passage says that today the job of handling mentally disturbed inmates is MAINLY   11._____
up to

A. psychiatric personnel   B. other inmates
C. correction officers   D. administrative officials

12. Of the following, which is a reason given in the passage for society's failure to provide adequate treatment programs for mentally disturbed inmates?   12.____

    A. Law-abiding citizens should not have to pay for fancy treatment programs for criminals.
    B. A person who breaks the law should not expect society to give him special help.
    C. It is impossible to tell whether an inmate is mentally disturbed.
    D. There are not enough trained people to provide the kind of treatment needed.

13. The expression *abnormal individual,* as used in the last sentence of the passage, refers to an individual who is   13.____

    A. of average intelligence   B. of superior intelligence
    C. completely normal   D. mentally disturbed

14. The reader of the passage would MOST likely agree that   14.____

    A. correction officers should not expect mentally disturbed persons to behave the same way a normal person would behave
    B. correction officers should not report infractions of the rules committed by mentally disturbed persons
    C. mentally disturbed persons who break the law should be treated exactly the same way as anyone else
    D. mentally disturbed persons who have broken the law should not be imprisoned

Questions 15-19.

DIRECTIONS: Questions 15 through 19 are to be answered SOLELY on the basis of the following paragraph.

When a young boy or girl is released from one of the various facilities operated by the Division for Youth, supportive services to help the youth face community, group, and family pressures are needed as much as, if not more than, at any other time. These services are the responsibility of two units of the Division for Youth, the Aftercare Unit, which serves youths discharged from the urban homes, camps, and START Centers, and the Community Service Bureaus, which serve youths released from the division's school and center programs. To assure that supportive services for released youths are easily identifiable and accessible, the division has developed the *store-front* services center, located in the heart of those areas to which many of the youngsters are returning. The storefront concept and structure is able to coordinate more closely services to the particular needs and situation of the youths and to draw on the feeling of community participation and achievement by persuading the community to join in helping them.

15. Of the following, the BEST description of the storefront services center's relationship to neighborhood residents is that it   15.____

    A. actively encourages their participation
    B. accepts their help when offered
    C. asks neighborhood residents to develop rehabilitation programs
    D. limits participation to qualified neighborhood professional youth workers

16. On the basis of the paragraph, which of the following statements is CORRECT? 16._____

    A. Supportive services are not needed as much after a youth is released from a facility as during his stay.
    B. Storefront services centers are located near the facilities operated by the Division for Youth.
    C. The Community Service Bureaus serve youths released from urban homes.
    D. Youths are given supportive services in their communities after release from facilities operated by the Division for Youth.

17. Of the following, the MOST suitable title for the above paragraph would be 17._____

    A. PROBLEMS OF YOUTHS RETURNING TO SOCIETY
    B. COMMUNITY, GROUP, AND FAMILY PRESSURES ON RELEASED YOUTHS
    C. NEIGHBORHOOD SUPPORTIVE SERVICES FOR RELEASED YOUTHS
    D. A SURVEY OF FACILITIES OPERATED BY THE DIVISION FOR YOUTH

18. Which of the following characteristics of the storefront services is mentioned in the above paragraph? 18._____

    A. Cost   B. Availability
    C. Size   D. Complexity

19. On the basis of the paragraph, which of the following statements about the Aftercare Unit is INCORRECT? 19._____
It

    A. is a part of the Division for Youth
    B. serves youths released from school programs
    C. is similar in function to the Community Service Bureaus
    D. was partly responsible for the development of storefront centers

20. The intended purposes of imprisonment are to punish, to correct through fear of repeated punishment, to provide opportunity for penitence, and to protect society by isolating the criminal. In point of fact, other emotions–notably hate for and a desire for revenge against those responsible for their imprisonment–are a greater product of imprisonment than is fear.
On the basis of this paragraph alone, the MOST accurate of the following conclusions is that 20._____

    A. a basis for further criminality is established by emotional factors resulting from previous imprisonment
    B. imprisonment will achieve its intended purpose only to the extent that it substitutes emotional reactions for logical thought
    C. opportunities for penitence are made more necessary by the growth of a desire for revenge
    D. society's protection is necessarily limited to the time an individual is imprisoned

21. The misconduct of juveniles is a symptom of some inner or outer disturbance, usually both. To the casual observer, his behavior may seem naughty or vicious, or both. To the delinquent himself, it has as much meaning as socially approved activity has for the well-behaved. Misconduct, according to this statement, 21._____

A. has meaning to the delinquent only if it carries with it strong social disapproval
B. is resorted to in many cases as an attention-getter device to impress the casual observer
C. may result from personal maladjustments and is meaningful to the delinquent
D. stems from a juvenile's rejection of social approval for his normal activities

Questions 22-25.

DIRECTIONS: Questions 22 through 25 are to be answered on the basis of the following passage.

There is controversy and misunderstanding about the proper function of juvenile courts and their probation departments. There are cries that the whole process produces delinquents rather than rehabilitates them. There are speeches by the score about *getting tough* with the kids. Another large group thinks we should be more understanding and gentle with delinquents. This distrust of the services offered can be attributed in large part to the confusion in the use of these services throughout the country.

On the one hand, the juvenile courts are tied to the criminal court system, with an obligation to decide guilt and innocence for offenses specifically stated and formally charged. On the other hand, they have the obligation to provide treatment, supervision, and guidance to youngsters in trouble, without respect to the crimes of which they are accused. These two conflicting assignments must be carried out – quite properly – in an informal, private way, which will not stigmatize a youngster during his formative years.

And, as the courts' preoccupation with the latter task has increased, the former (that of dispensing justice) has retreated, with the result that grave injustices are bound to occur.

22. The title below that BEST expresses the ideas of this passage is   22.___

    A. A PROBLEM FOR TODAY'S TEENAGERS
    B. REHABILITATING YOUTHFUL CRIMINALS
    C. FITTING THE PUNISHMENT TO THE CRIME
    D. JUSTICE FOR JUVENILE OFFENDERS

23. The author contends that public distrust of juvenile courts is PRIMARILY the result of   23.___

    A. the dual function of these courts
    B. lack of a sufficient number of probation officers
    C. injustices done by the courts
    D. the cost of keeping up the courts

24. The passage suggests that the author   24.___

    A. is familiar with the problem
    B. is impatient with justice
    C. sides with those who favor leniency for juvenile offenders
    D. regards all offenses as equally important

25. The tone of the above passage is   25.___

    A. highly emotional   B. highly personal
    C. optimistic   D. calm

KEY (CORRECT ANSWERS)

1.	B		11.	C
2.	A		12.	D
3.	C		13.	D
4.	D		14.	A
5.	A		15.	A
6.	A		16.	D
7.	C		17.	C
8.	C		18.	B
9.	C		19.	B
10.	C		20.	A

21.	C
22.	D
23.	A
24.	A
25.	D

———

EXAMINATION SECTION
TEST 1

DIRECTIONS: Each question or incomplete statement is followed by several suggested answers or completions. Select the one that BEST answers the question or completes the statement. *PRINT THE LETTER OF THE CORRECT ANSWER IN THE SPACE AT THE RIGHT.*

Questions 1-4.

DIRECTIONS: Questions 1 to 4 measure your ability (1) to determine whether statements from witnesses say essentially the same thing and (2) to determine the evidence needed to make it reasonably certain that a particular conclusion is true.

To do well in this part of the test, you do NOT have to have a working knowledge of police procedures and techniques or to have any more familiarity with crimes and criminal behavior than that acquired from reading newspapers, listening to radio, or watching TV. To do well in this part, you must read carefully and reason closely. Sloppy reading or sloppy reasoning will lead to a low score.

1. In which of the following do the two statements made say essentially the same thing in two different ways?
    I. All members of the pro-x group are free from persecution. No person that is persecuted is a member of the pro-x group.
    II. Some responsible employees of the police department are not supervisors. Some police department supervisors are not responsible employees.
   The CORRECT answer is:

   A. I *only*
   C. Both I and II
   B. II *only*
   D. Neither I nor II

   1.____

2. In which of the following do the two statements made say essentially the same thing in two different ways?
    I. All Nassau County police officers weigh less than 225 pounds.
    II. No police officer weighs more than 225 pounds.
       No police officer is an alcoholic. No alcoholic is a police officer.
   The CORRECT answer is:

   A. I *only*
   C. Both I and II
   B. II *only*
   D. Neither I nor II

   2.____

3. Summary of Evidence Collected to Date: All pimps in the precinct own pink-colored cars and carry knives.
   Prematurely Drawn Conclusion: Any person in the precinct who carries a knife is a pimp.
   Which one of the following additional pieces of evidence, if any, would make it *reasonably certain* that the conclusion drawn is TRUE?

   A. Each person who carries a knife owns a pink-colored car.
   B. All persons who own pink-colored cars pimp.

   3.____

    C.   No one who carries a knife has a vocation other than pimping.
    D.   None of these

4.   Summary of Evidence Collected to Date: 4.___
     1.   Some of the robbery suspects have served time as convicted felons.
     2.   Some of the robbery suspects are female.
     Prematurely Drawn Conclusion: Some of the female suspects have never served time
     as convicted felons.
     Which one of the following additional pieces of evidence, if any, would make it *reasonably certain* that the conclusion drawn is TRUE?

    A.   The number of female suspects is the same as the number of robbery suspects
         who have served time as convicted felons.
    B.   The number of female suspects is smaller than the number of convicted felons.
    C.   The number of suspects that have served time is smaller than the number of suspects that have been convicted of a felony.
    D.   None of these

Questions 5-8.

DIRECTIONS: Questions 5 to 8 measure your ability to orient yourself within a given section
              of a town, neighborhood, or particular area. Each of the questions describes a
              starting point and a destination. Assume that you are driving a patrol car in the
              area shown on the map accompanying the questions. Use the map as a basis
              for choosing the shortest way to get from one point to another without breaking
              the law.

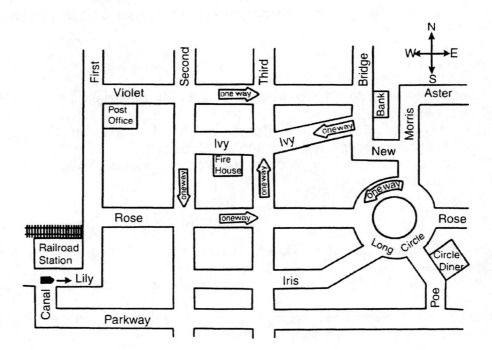

A street marked *one way* is one-way for the full length, even when there are breaks or jogs in
the street. EXCEPTION: A street that does not have the same name over the full length.

5. A patrol car at the train station is sent to the bank to investigate a robbery. The SHORT-EST way to get there without breaking any traffic laws is to go

    5.____

    A.   east on Lily, north on First, east on Rose, north on Third, and east on Ivy to bank
    B.   east on Lily, north on First, east on Violet, and south on Bridge to bank
    C.   south on Canal, east on Parkway, north on Poe, around Long Circle to Morris, west on New, and north on Bridge to bank
    D.   south on Canal, east on Parkway, north on Third, and east on Ivy to bank

6. At the bank, the patrol car receives a call to hurry to the post office. The SHORTEST way to get there without breaking any traffic laws is to go

    6.____

    A.   west on Ivy, south on Second, west on Rose, and north on First to post office
    B.   west on Ivy, south on Second, west on Rose, and south on First to post office
    C.   south on Bridge, east on New, south on Morris, around Long Circle, south on Poe, west on Parkway, north on Canal, east on Lily, and north on First to post office
    D.   north on Bridge, west on Violet, and south on First to post office.

7. On leaving the post office, the police officers decide to go to the Circle Diner. The SHORTEST way to get there without breaking any traffic laws is to go

    7.____

    A.   south on First, left on Rose, right on Second, left on Parkway, and right on Poe to diner
    B.   south on First, left on Rose, around Long Circle, and right on Poe to diner
    C.   south on First, left on Rose, right on Second, right on Iris, around Long Circle, and left on Poe to diner
    D.   west on Violet, right on Bridge, right on New, right on Morris, around Long Circle, and left on Poe to diner

8. During lunch break, a fire siren sounds and the police officers rush to their patrol car and head for the fire-house. The SHORTEST way to get there without breaking any traffic laws is to go

    8.____

    A.   north on Poe, around Long Circle, west on Iris, north on Third, and west on Ivy to firehouse
    B.   north on Poe, around Long Circle, north on Morris, west on New, north on Bridge, and west on Ivy to firehouse
    C.   north on Poe, around Long Circle, west on Rose, north on Third, and west on Ivy to firehouse
    D.   south on Poe, west on Parkway, north on Third, and east on Ivy to firehouse

Questions 9-13.

DIRECTIONS: Questions 9 to 13 measure your ability to understand written descriptions of events. Each question presents you with a description of an accident, a crime, or an event and asks you which of four drawings BEST represent it.

In the drawings, the following symbols are used (these symbols and their meanings will be repeated in the test):

A moving vehicle is represented by this symbol: (front) ⬠ (rear)

A parked vehicle is represented by this symbol: (front) ◀ (rear)

A pedestrian or a bicyclist is represented by this symbol: •

The path and direction of travel of a vehicle or pedestrian is indicated by a solid line: ⟶

EXCEPTION: The path and direction of travel of each vehicle or person directly involved in a collision from the point of impact is indicated by a dotted line: --⟶

9. A driver pulling out from between two parked cars on Magic is struck by a vehicle heading east which turns left onto Maple and flees.
Which of the following depicts the accident?

9._

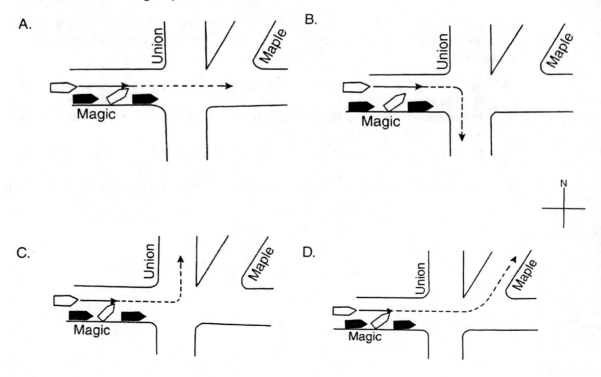

10. As Mr. Jones is driving south on Side. St., he falls asleep at the wheel. His car goes out of control and sideswipes an oncoming car, goes through an intersection, and hits a pedestrian on the southeast corner of Main Street.
Which of the following depicts the accident?

10.____

A.

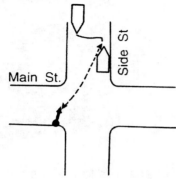

B.

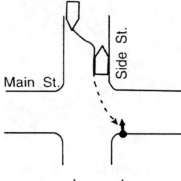

C.

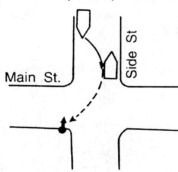

D.

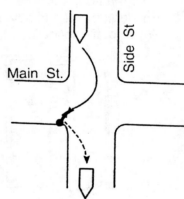

11. A car traveling south on Baltic skids through a red light at the intersection of Baltic and Atlantic, sideswipes a car stopped for a light in the northbound lane, skids 180 degrees, and stops on the west sidewalk of Baltic.
Which of the following depicts the accident?

11.____

A.

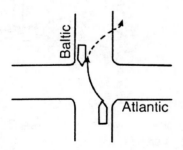

B.

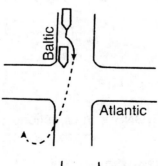

C.

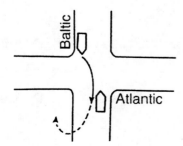

D.

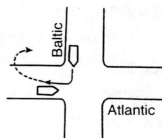

12. When found, the right front end of an automobile was smashed and bent around a post, and the hood was buckled.
Which of the following cars on a service lot is the car described?

12.

A.

B.

C.

D.

13. An open floor safe with its door bent out of shape was found at the scene. It was empty. An electric drill and several envelopes and papers were found on the floor near the safe.
Which of the following shows the scene described?

13.

A.

B.

C.

D.

Questions 14-16.

DIRECTIONS: In Questions 14 to 16, you are to pick the word or phrase CLOSEST in meaning to the word or phrase printed in capital letters.

14. HAZARDOUS

14

    A. uncertain   B. threatening   C. difficult   D. dangerous

15. NEGLIGENT

15.

    A. careless   B. fearless   C. ruthless   D. useless

16. PROVOKE

16

    A. accuse   B. arouse   C. insist   D. suspend

Questions 17-20.

DIRECTIONS: Questions 17 to 20 measure your ability to do arithmetic related to police work.
Each question presents a separate arithmetic problem to be solved.

17. To the nearest hour, how long can a specialized police vehicle with a 40-gallon fuel tank   17.____
be on the road before heading for a service facility, assuming that the vehicle consumes
8 gallons per hour and must head for a service facility when there are only 8 gallons in
the tank?

   A. 3   B. 4   C. 5   D.   None of these

18. A man with a history of vagrancy was found dead under a bridge with the following U.S.   18.____
currency in a band around his belly:
               7    $5   bills
               3   $10   bills
              11   $20   bills
               9   $50   bills
               4 $100   bills
What is the total amount of the money that was found in the band?

   A. $1,015   B. $1,135   C. $2,710   D.   None of these

19. X is 110 dimes.   19.____
Y is 1,111 pennies.
Which of the following statements about the values of X and Y above is TRUE?

   A.   X is greater than Y.
   B.   Y is greater than X.
   C.   X equals Y.
   D.   The relationship of X to Y cannot be determined from the information given.

20. Which of the following individuals drinking hard liquor in a bar was 21 years old at the   20.____
time of the incident?

   A.   One born August 26, 1989 - Date of incident is March 17, 2010
   B.   One born January 6, 1989 - Date of incident is New Year's Eve 2009
   C.   One born 3/17/89 - Date of incident is 2/14/10
   D.   None of these

———

KEY (CORRECT ANSWERS)

1.	A	11.	C
2.	B	12.	D
3.	C	13.	B
4.	D	14.	D
5.	B	15.	A
6.	C	16.	B
7.	B	17.	B
8.	B	18.	B
9.	D	19.	B
10.	B	20.	D

———

EXAMINATION SECTION
TEST 1

Directions: Each question or incomplete statement is followed by several suggested answers or completions. Select the one that BEST answers the question or completes the statement. *PRINT THE LETTER OF THE CORRECT ANSWER IN THE SPACE AT THE RIGHT.*

Questions 1-9.

DIRECTIONS: In questions 1-9, you will read a set of facts and a conclusion drawn from them. The conclusion may be valid or invalid, based on the facts—it's your task to determine the validity of the conclusion.

For each question, select the letter before the statement that BEST expresses the relationship between the given facts and the conclusion that has been drawn from them. Your choices are:

    A.   The facts prove the conclusion
    B.   The facts disprove the conclusion; or
    C.   The facts neither prove nor disprove the conclusion.

1)   FACTS: Lauren must use Highway 29 to get to work. Lauren has a meeting today at 9:00 am. If she misses the meeting, Lauren will probably lose a major account. Highway 29 is closed all day today for repairs.

1. _____

CONCLUSION: Lauren will not be able to get to work.

A.   The facts prove the conclusion.
B.   The facts disprove the conclusion.
C.   The facts neither prove nor disprove the conclusion.

2)   FACTS: The Tumbleweed Follies, a traveling burlesque show, is looking for a new line dancer. The position requires both singing and dancing skills. If the show cannot fill the position by Friday, it will begin to look for a magician to fill the time slot currently held by the line dancers. Willa, who wants to audition for the line dancing position, can sing, but cannot dance.

2. _____

CONCLUSION: Willa is qualified to audition for the part of line dancer.

A.   The facts prove the conclusion.
B.   The facts disprove the conclusion.
C.   The facts neither prove nor disprove the conclusion.

3)   FACTS: Terry owns two dogs, Spike and Stan. One of the dogs is short-haired and has blue eyes. One dog has a pink nose. The blue-eyed dog never barks. One of the dogs has white fur on its paws. Sam has long hair.

3. _____

CONCLUSION: Spike never barks.

A.   The facts prove the conclusion.
B.   The facts disprove the conclusion.
C.   The facts neither prove nor disprove the conclusion.

4)   FACTS: No science teachers are members of the PTA. Some English teachers are members of the PTA. Some English teachers in the PTA also wear glasses. Every PTA member is required to sit on the dunking stool at the student carnival except for those who wear glasses, who will be exempt. Those who are exempt, however, will have to officiate the hamster races. All of the English teachers in the PTA who do not wear glasses are married.

4. _____

CONCLUSION: All the married English teachers in the PTA will sit on the dunking stool at the student carnival.

A.   The facts prove the conclusion.
B.   The facts disprove the conclusion.
C.   The facts neither prove nor disprove the conclusion.

5)   FACTS: If the price of fuel is increased and sales remain constant, oil company profits will increase. The price of fuel was increased, and market experts project that sales levels are likely to be maintained.

5. _____

CONCLUSION: The price of fuel will increase.

A.   The facts prove the conclusion.
B.   The facts disprove the conclusion.
C.   The facts neither prove nor disprove the conclusion.

6)   FACTS: Some members of the gymnastics team are double-jointed, and some members of the gymnastics team are also on the lacrosse team. Some double-jointed members of the gymnastics team are also coaches. All gymnastics team members perform floor exercises, except the coaches. All the double-jointed members of the gymnastics team who are not coaches are freshmen.

6. _____

CONCLUSION: Some double-jointed freshmen are coaches.

A.   The facts prove the conclusion.
B.   The facts disprove the conclusion.
C.   The facts neither prove nor disprove the conclusion.

7)   FACTS: Each member of the International Society speaks at least one foreign language, but no member speaks more than four foreign languages. Five members speak Spanish; three speak Mandarin; four speak French; four speak German; and five speak a foreign language other than Spanish, Mandarin, French, or German.

7. _____

CONCLUSION: The lowest possible number of members in the International Society is eight.

A.   The facts prove the conclusion.
B.   The facts disprove the conclusion.
C.   The facts neither prove nor disprove the conclusion.

8)   FACTS: Mary keeps seven cats in her apartment. Only three of the cats will eat the same kind of food. Mary wants to keep at least one extra bag of each kind of food.

8. _____

CONCLUSION: The minimum number of bags Mary will need to keep as extra is 7.

A.   The facts prove the conclusion.
B.   The facts disprove the conclusion.
C.   The facts neither prove nor disprove the conclusion.

9)   FACTS: In Ed and Marie's exercise group, everyone likes the treadmill or the stationary bicycle, or both, but Ed does not like the stationary bicycle. Marie has not expressed a preference, but spends most of her time on the stationary bicycle.

9. _____

CONCLUSION: Everyone in the group who does not like the treadmill likes the stationary bicycle.

A.   The facts prove the conclusion.
B.   The facts disprove the conclusion.
C.   The facts neither prove nor disprove the conclusion.

Questions 10-17.

DIRECTIONS: Questions 10-17 are based on the following reading passage. It is not your knowledge of the particular topic that is being tested, but your ability to reason based on what you have read. The passage is likely to detail several proposed courses of action and factors affecting these proposals. The reading passage is followed by a conclusion or outcome based on the facts in the passage, or a description of a decision taken regarding the situation. The conclusion is followed by a number of statements that have a possible connection to the conclusion. For each statement, you are to determine whether:

    A.   The statement proves the conclusion.
    B.   The statement supports the conclusion but does not prove it.
    C.   The statement disproves the conclusion.
    D.   The statement weakens the conclusion but does not disprove it.
    E.   The statement has no relevance to the conclusion.

Remember that the conclusion after the passage is to be accepted as the outcome of what actually happened, and that you are being asked to evaluate the impact each statement would have had on the conclusion.

PASSAGE:

       The Owyhee Mission School District's Board of Directors is hosting a public meeting to debate the merits of the proposed abolition of all bilingual education programs within the district. The group that has made the proposal believes the programs, which teach immigrant children academic subjects in their native language until they have learned English well enough to join mainstream classes, inhibit the ability of students to acquire English quickly and succeed in school and in the larger American society. Such programs, they argue, are also a wasteful drain on the district's already scant resources.

       At the meeting, several teachers and parents stand to speak out against the proposal. The purpose of an education, they say, should be to build upon, rather than dismantle, a minority child's language and culture. By teaching children in academic subjects in their native tongues, while simultaneously offering English language instruction, schools can meet the goals of learning English and progressing through academic subjects along with their peers.

       Hiram Nguyen, a representative of the parents whose children are currently enrolled in bilingual education, stands at the meeting to express the parents' wishes. The parents have been polled, he says, and are overwhelmingly of the opinion that while language and culture are important to them, they are not things that will disappear from the students' lives if they are no longer taught in the classroom. The most important issue for the parents is whether their children will succeed in school and be competitive in the larger American society. If bilingual education can be demonstrated to do that, then the parents are in favor of continuing it.

At the end of the meeting, a proponent of the plan, Oscar Ramos, stands to clarify some misconceptions about the proposal. It does not call for a "sink or swim" approach, he says, but allows for an interpreter to be present in mainstream classes to explain anything a student finds too complex or confusing.

The last word of the meeting is given to Delia Cruz, a bilingual teacher at one of the district's elementary schools. A student is bound to find anything complex or confusing, she says, if it is spoken in a language he has never heard before. It is more wasteful to place children in classrooms where they don't understand anything, she says, than it is to try to teach them something useful as they are learning the English language.

CONCLUSION: After the meeting, the Owyhee Mission School District's Board of Directors votes to terminate all the district's bilingual education programs at the end of the current academic year, but to maintain the current level of funding to each of the schools that have programs cut.

10) A poll conducted by the *Los Angeles Times* at approximately the same time as the Board's meeting indicated that 75% of the people were opposed to bilingual education; among Latinos, opposition was 84%.

10. _____

A.
B.
C.
D.
E.

11) Of all the studies conducted on bilingual education programs, 64% indicate that students learned English grammar better in "sink or swim" classes without any special features than they did in bilingual education classes.

11. _____

A.
B.
C.
D.
E.

12) In the academic year that begins after the Board's vote, Montgomery Burns Elementary, an Owyhee Mission District school, launches a new bilingual program for the children of Somali immigrants.

12. _____

A.
B.
C.
D.
E.

13)   In the previous academic year, under severe budget restraints, the Owyhee Mission District cut all physical education, music, and art classes, but its
funding for bilingual education classes increased by 18%.

13. _____

A.
B.
C.
D.
E.

14)   Before the Board votes, a polling consultant conducts randomly
sampled assessments of immigrant students who enrolled in Owyhee district
schools at a time when they did not speak any English at all. Ten years after
graduating from high school, 44% of those who received bilingual instruction
were professionals—doctors, lawyers, educators, engineers, etc. Of those who
did not receive bilingual education, 38% were professionals.

14. _____

A.
B.
C.
D.
E.

15)   Over the past several years, the scores of Owyhee District students
have gradually declined, and enrollment numbers have followed as anxious
parents transferred their children to other schools or applied for a state-funded
voucher program.

15. _____

A.
B.
C.
D.
E.

16)   California and Massachusetts, two of the most liberal states in the
country, have each passed ballot measures banning bilingual education in public schools.

16. _____

A.
B.
C.
D.
E.

17)   In the academic year that begins after the Board's vote, no Owyhee   17. _____
Mission District Schools are conducting bilingual instruction.

A.
B.
C.
D.
E.

Questions 18-25.

DIRECTIONS: Questions 18-25 each provide four factual statements and a
conclusion based on these statements. After reading the entire question, you
will decide whether:

      A.   The conclusion is proved by statements 1-4;
      B.   The conclusion is disproved by statements 1-4; or
      C.   The facts are not sufficient to prove or disprove the conclusion.

18)   FACTUAL STATEMENTS: 18. _____

1.   Gear X rotates in a clockwise direction if Switch C is in the OFF position
2.   Gear X will rotate in a counter-clockwise direction if Switch C is ON.
3.   If Gear X is rotating in a clockwise direction, then Gear Y will not be
rotating at all.
4.   Switch C is OFF.

CONCLUSION: Gear Y is rotating.

A.   The conclusion is proved by statements 1-4.
B.   The conclusion is disproved by statements 1-4.
C.   The facts are not sufficient to prove or disprove the conclusion.

19)   FACTUAL STATEMENTS: 19. _____

1.   Mark is older than Jim but younger than Dan.
2.   Fern is older than Mark but younger than Silas.
3.   Dan is younger than Silas but older than Edward.
4.   Edward is older than Mark but younger than Fern.

CONCLUSION: Dan is older than Fern.

A.   The conclusion is proved by statements 1-4.
B.   The conclusion is disproved by statements 1-4.
C.   The facts are not sufficient to prove or disprove the conclusion.

20) FACTUAL STATEMENTS: 20. _____

1.   Each of Fred's three sofa cushions lies on top of four lost coins.
2.   The cushion on the right covers two pennies and two dimes.
3.   The middle cushion covers two dimes and two quarters.
4.   The cushion on the left covers two nickels and two quarters.

CONCLUSION: To be guaranteed of retrieving at least one coin of each denomination, and without looking at any of the coins, Frank must take three coins each from under the cushions on the right and the left.

A.   The conclusion is proved by statements 1-4.
B.   The conclusion is disproved by statements 1-4.
C.   The facts are not sufficient to prove or disprove the conclusion.

21) FACTUAL STATEMENTS: 21. _____

1.   The door to the hammer mill chamber is locked if light 6 is red.
2.   The door to the hammer mill chamber is locked only when the mill is operating.
3.   If the mill is not operating, light 6 is blue.
4.   The door to the hammer mill chamber is locked.

CONCLUSION: The mill is in operation.

A.   The conclusion is proved by statements 1-4.
B.   The conclusion is disproved by statements 1-4.
C.   The facts are not sufficient to prove or disprove the conclusion.

22) FACTUAL STATEMENTS: 22. _____

1.   In a five-story office building, where each story is occupied by a single professional, Dr. Kane's office is above Dr. Assad's.
2.   Dr. Johnson's office is between Dr. Kane's and Dr. Conlon's.
3.   Dr. Steen's office is between Dr. Conlon's and Dr. Assad's.
4.   Dr. Johnson is on the fourth story.

CONCLUSION: Dr. Steen occupies the second story.

A.   The conclusion is proved by statements 1-4.
B.   The conclusion is disproved by statements 1-4.
C.   The facts are not sufficient to prove or disprove the conclusion.

23) FACTUAL STATEMENTS: 23. _____

1.   On Saturday, farmers Hank, Earl, Roy, and Cletus plowed a total of 520 acres.
2.   Hank plowed twice as many acres as Roy.
3.   Roy plowed half as much as the farmer who plowed the most.
4.   Cletus plowed 160 acres.

CONCLUSION: Hank plowed 200 acres.

A.   The conclusion is proved by statements 1-4.
B.   The conclusion is disproved by statements 1-4.
C.   The facts are not sufficient to prove or disprove the conclusion.

24) FACTUAL STATEMENTS: 24. _____

1.   Four travelers—Tina, Jodie, Alex, and Oscar—each traveled to a different island—Aruba, Jamaica, Nevis, and Barbados—but not necessarily respectively.
2.   Tina did not travel as far to Jamaica as Jodie traveled to her island.
3.   Oscar traveled twice as far as Alex, who traveled the same distance as the traveler who went to Aruba.
4.   Oscar went to Barbados.

CONCLUSION: Oscar traveled the farthest.

A.   The conclusion is proved by statements 1-4.
B.   The conclusion is disproved by statements 1-4.
C.   The facts are not sufficient to prove or disprove the conclusion.

25) FACTUAL STATEMENTS: 25. _____

1.   In the natural history museum, every Native American display that contains pottery also contains beadwork.
2.   Some of the displays containing lodge replicas also contain beadwork.
3.   The display on the Choctaw, a Native American tribe, contains pottery.
4.   The display on the Modoc, a Native American tribe, contains only two of these items.

CONCLUSION: If the Modoc display contains pottery, it does not contain lodge replicas.

A.   The conclusion is proved by statements 1-4.
B.   The conclusion is disproved by statements 1-4.
C.   The facts are not sufficient to prove or disprove the conclusion.

KEY (CORRECT ANSWERS)

1. A
2. B
3. A
4. A
5. C

6. B
7. B
8. B
9. A
10. B

11. B
12. C
13. B
14. D
15. E

16. E
17. A
18. B
19. C
20. A

21. A
22. A
23. C
24. A
25. A

TEST 2

Directions: Each question or incomplete statement is followed by several suggested answers or completions. Select the one that BEST answers the question or completes the statement. *PRINT THE LETTER OF THE CORRECT ANSWER IN THE SPACE AT THE RIGHT.*

Questions 1-9.

DIRECTIONS: In questions 1-9, you will read a set of facts and a conclusion drawn from them. The conclusion may be valid or invalid, based on the facts—it's your task to determine the validity of the conclusion.

For each question, select the letter before the statement that BEST expresses the relationship between the given facts and the conclusion that has been drawn from them. Your choices are:

    A.   The facts prove the conclusion
    B.   The facts disprove the conclusion; or
    C.   The facts neither prove nor disprove the conclusion.

1)   FACTS: If the maximum allowable income for Medicaid recipients is increased, the number of Medicaid recipients will increase. If the number of Medicaid recipients increases, more funds must be allocated to the Medicaid program, which will require a tax increase. Taxes cannot be approved without the approval of the legislature. The legislature probably will not approve a tax increase.

CONCLUSION: The maximum allowable income for Medicaid recipients will increase.

1. _____

A.   The facts prove the conclusion.
B.   The facts disprove the conclusion.
C.   The facts neither prove nor disprove the conclusion.

2)   FACTS: All the dentists on the baseball team are short. Everyone in the dugout is a dentist, but not everyone in the dugout is short. The baseball team is not made up of people of any particular profession.

CONCLUSION: Some people who are not dentists are in the dugout.

2. _____

A.   The facts prove the conclusion.
B.   The facts disprove the conclusion.
C.   The facts neither prove nor disprove the conclusion.

3)   FACTS: A taxi company's fleet is divided into two fleets. Fleet One   3. _____
contains cabs A, B, C, and D. Fleet Two contains E, F, G, and H. Each cab is
either yellow or green. Five of the cabs are yellow. Cabs A and E are not both
yellow. Either Cab C or F, or both, are not yellow. Cabs B and H are either
both yellow or both green.

CONCLUSION: Cab H is green.

A.   The facts prove the conclusion.
B.   The facts disprove the conclusion.
C.   The facts neither prove nor disprove the conclusion.

4)   FACTS: Most people in the skydiving club are not afraid of heights.   4. _____
Everyone in the skydiving club makes three parachute jumps a month.

CONCLUSION: At least one person who is afraid of heights makes three
parachute jumps a month.

A.   The facts prove the conclusion.
B.   The facts disprove the conclusion.
C.   The facts neither prove nor disprove the conclusion.

5)   FACTS: If the Board approves the new rule, the agency will move to a   5. _____
new location immediately. If the agency moves, five new supervisors will be
immediately appointed. The Board has approved the new proposal.

CONCLUSION: No new supervisors were appointed.

A.   The facts prove the conclusion.
B.   The facts disprove the conclusion.
C.   The facts neither prove nor disprove the conclusion.

6)   FACTS: All the workers at the supermarket chew gum when they sack   6. _____
groceries. Sometimes Lance, a supermarket worker, doesn't chew gum at all
when he works. Another supermarket worker, Jenny, chews gum the whole
time she is at work.

CONCLUSION: Jenny always sacks groceries when she is at work.

A.   The facts prove the conclusion.
B.   The facts disprove the conclusion.
C.   The facts neither prove nor disprove the conclusion.

7)   FACTS: Lake Lottawatta is bigger than Lake Tacomi. Lake Tacomi   7. _____
and Lake Ottawa are exactly the same size. All lakes in Montana are bigger
than Lake Ottawa.

CONCLUSION: Lake Lottawatta is in Montana.

A.   The facts prove the conclusion.
B.   The facts disprove the conclusion.
C.   The facts neither prove nor disprove the conclusion.

8)   FACTS: Two men, Cox and Taylor, are playing poker at a table. Tay-   8. _____
lor has a pair of aces in his hand. One man is smoking a cigar. One of them
has no pairs in his hand and is wearing an eye patch. The man wearing the
eye patch is smoking a cigar. One man is bald.

CONCLUSION: Cox is smoking a cigar.

A.   The facts prove the conclusion.
B.   The facts disprove the conclusion.
C.   The facts neither prove nor disprove the conclusion.

9)   FACTS: All Kwakiutls are Wakashan Indians. All Wakashan Indians   9. _____
originated on Vancouver Island. The Nootka also originated on Vancouver
Island.

CONCLUSION: Kwakiutls originated on Vancouver Island.

A.   The facts prove the conclusion.
B.   The facts disprove the conclusion.
C.   The facts neither prove nor disprove the conclusion.

Questions 10-17.

DIRECTIONS: Questions 10-17 are based on the following reading passage. It is not your knowledge of the particular topic that is being tested, but your ability to reason based on what you have read. The passage is likely to detail several proposed courses of action and factors affecting these proposals. The reading passage is followed by a conclusion or outcome based on the facts in the passage, or a description of a decision taken regarding the situation. The conclusion is followed by a number of statements that have a possible connection to the conclusion. For each statement, you are to determine whether:

A. The statement proves the conclusion.
B. The statement supports the conclusion but does not prove it.
C. The statement disproves the conclusion.
D. The statement weakens the conclusion but does not disprove it.
E. The statement has no relevance to the conclusion.

Remember that the conclusion after the passage is to be accepted as the outcome of what actually happened, and that you are being asked to evaluate the impact each statement would have had on the conclusion.

PASSAGE:

The World Wide Web portal and search engine. HipBot, is considering becoming a subscription-only service, locking out nonsubscribers from the content on its Web site. HipBot currently relies solely on advertising revenues.

HipBot's content director says that by taking in an annual fee from each customer, the company can both increase profits and provide premium content that no other portal can match.

The marketing director disagrees, saying that there is no guarantee that anyone who now visits the Web site for free will agree to pay for the privilege of visiting it again. Most will probably simply use of the other major portals. Also, HipBot's advertising clients will not be happy when they learn that the site will be viewed by a more limited number of people.

CONCLUSION: In January of 2010, the CEO of HipBot decides to keep the portal open to all Web users, with some limited "premium content" available to subscribers who don't mind paying a little extra to access it. The company will aim to maintain, or perhaps increase, its advertising revenue.

10) In an independent marketing survey, 62% of respondents said they   10. _____
"strongly agree" with the following statement: "I almost never pay attention to
advertisements that appear on the World Wide Web."

A.
B.
C.
D.
E.

11) When it learns about the subscription-only debate going on at HipBot,   11. _____
Wernham Hogg Entertainment, one of HipBot's most reliable clients, says it
will withdraw its ads and place them on a free Web portal if HipBot decides to
limit its content to subscribers. Wernham Hogg pays HipBot about $6 million
annually—about 12% of HipBot's gross revenues—to run its ads online.

A.
B.
C.
D.
E.

12) At the end of the second quarter of FY 2010, after continued stagnant   12. _____
profits, the CEO of HipBot assembles a blue ribbon commission to gather and
analyze data on the costs, benefits, and feasibility of adding a limited amount
of "premium" content to the HipBot portal.

A.
B.
C.
D.
E.

13) In the following fiscal year, Wernham Hogg Entertainment, satisfied   13. _____
with the "hit counts" on HipBot's free Web site, spends another $1 million on
advertisements that will appear on Web pages that are available to HipBot's
"premium" subscribers.

A.
B.
C.
D.
E.

14)   HipBot's information technology director reports that the engineers in his department have come up with a feature that will search not only individual web pages, but tie into other Web-based search engines, as well, and then comb through all these results to find those most relevant to the user's search.

14. _____

A.
B.
C.
D.
E.

15)   In an independent marketing survey, 79% of respondents said they "strongly agree" with the following statement: "Many Web sites are so dominated by advertisements these days that it is increasingly frustrating to find the content I want to read or see."

15. _____

A.
B.
C.
D.
E.

16)   After three years of studies at the federal level, the Department of Commerce releases a report suggesting that in general, the only private "subscriber-only" Web sites that do well financially are those with a very specialized user population.

16. _____

A.
B.
C.
D.
E.

17)   HipBot's own marketing research indicates that the introduction of premium content has the potential to attract new users to the HipBot portal.

17. _____

A.
B.
C.
D.
E.

Questions 18-25.

DIRECTIONS: Questions 18-25 each provide four factual statements and a conclusion based on these statements. After reading the entire question, you will decide whether:

A.   The conclusion is proved by statements 1-4;
B.   The conclusion is disproved by statements 1-4; or
C.   The facts are not sufficient to prove or disprove the conclusion.

18)   FACTUAL STATEMENTS: 18. _____

1.   If the alarm goes off, Sam will wake up.
2.   If Tandy wakes up before 4:00, Linda will leave the bedroom and sleep on the couch.
3.   If Linda leaves the bedroom, she'll check the alarm to make sure it is working.
4.   The alarm goes off.

CONCLUSION: Tandy woke up before 4:00.

A.   The conclusion is proved by statements 1-4.
B.   The conclusion is disproved by statements 1-4.
C.   The facts are not sufficient to prove or disprove the conclusion.

19)   FACTUAL STATEMENTS: 19. _____

1.   Four brothers are named Earl, John, Gary, and Pete.
2.   Earl and Pete are unmarried.
3.   John is shorter than the youngest of the four.
4.   The oldest brother is married, and is also the tallest.

CONCLUSION: Pete is the youngest brother.

A.   The conclusion is proved by statements 1-4.
B.   The conclusion is disproved by statements 1-4.
C.   The facts are not sufficient to prove or disprove the conclusion.

20) FACTUAL STATEMENTS: 20. _____

1.   Automobile engines are cooled either by air or by liquid.
2.   If the engine is small and simple enough, air from a belt-driven fan will cool it sufficiently.
3.   Most newer automobile engines are too complicated to be air-cooled.
4.   Air-cooled engines are cheaper and easier to build than liquid-cooled engines.

CONCLUSION: Most newer automobile engines use liquid coolant.

A.   The conclusion is proved by statements 1-4.
B.   The conclusion is disproved by statements 1-4.
C.   The facts are not sufficient to prove or disprove the conclusion.

21) FACTUAL STATEMENTS: 21. _____

1.   Erica will only file a lawsuit if she is injured while parasailing.
2.   If Rick orders Trip to run a rope test, Trip will check the rigging.
3.   If the rigging does not malfunction, Erica will not be injured.
4.   Rick order Trip to run a rope test.

CONCLUSION: Erica does not file a lawsuit.

A.   The conclusion is proved by statements 1-4.
B.   The conclusion is disproved by statements 1-4.
C.   The facts are not sufficient to prove or disprove the conclusion.

22) FACTUAL STATEMENTS: 22. _____

1.   On Maple Street, which is four blocks long, Bill's shop is two blocks east of Ken's shop.
2.   Ken's shop is one block west of the only shop on Maple Street with an awning.
3.   Erma's shop is one block west of the easternmost block.
4.   Bill's shop is on the easternmost block.

CONCLUSION: Bill's shop has an awning.

A.   The conclusion is proved by statements 1-4.
B.   The conclusion is disproved by statements 1-4.
C.   The facts are not sufficient to prove or disprove the conclusion.

23)   FACTUAL STATEMENTS: 23. _____

1.   Gear X rotates in a clockwise direction if Switch C is in the OFF position

2.   Gear X will rotate in a counter-clockwise direction if Switch C is ON.
3.   If Gear X is rotating in a clockwise direction, then Gear Y will not be rotating at all.
4.   Gear Y is rotating.

CONCLUSION: Gear X is rotating in a counter-clockwise direction.

A.   The conclusion is proved by statements 1-4.
B.   The conclusion is disproved by statements 1-4.
C.   The facts are not sufficient to prove or disprove the conclusion.

24)   FACTUAL STATEMENTS: 24. _____

1.   The Republic of Garbanzo's currency system has four basic denominations: the pastor, the noble, the donner, and the rojo.
2.   A pastor is worth 2 nobles.
3.   2 donners can be exchanged for a rojo.
4.   3 pastors are equal in value to 2 donners.

CONCLUSION: The rojo is most valuable.

A.   The conclusion is proved by statements 1-4.
B.   The conclusion is disproved by statements 1-4.
C.   The facts are not sufficient to prove or disprove the conclusion.

25)   FACTUAL STATEMENTS: 25. _____

1.   At Prickett's Nursery, the only citrus trees left are either Meyer lemons or Valencia oranges, and every citrus tree left is either a dwarf or a semidwarf.
2.   Half of the semidwarf trees are Meyer lemons.
3.   There are more semidwarf trees left than dwarf trees.
4.   A quarter of the dwarf trees are Valencia oranges.

CONCLUSION: There are more Valencia oranges left at Prickett's Nursery than Meyer lemons.

A.   The conclusion is proved by statements 1-4.
B.   The conclusion is disproved by statements 1-4.
C.   The facts are not sufficient to prove or disprove the conclusion.

KEY (CORRECT ANSWERS)

1. C
2. B
3. B
4. A
5. B

6. C
7. C
8. A
9. A
10. E

11. B
12. C
13. A
14. E
15. D

16. B
17. B
18. C
19. C
20. A

21. C
22. B
23. C
24. A
25. B

REPORT WRITING

EXAMINATION SECTION
TEST 1

DIRECTIONS: Each question or incomplete statement is followed by several suggested answers or completions. Select the one that BEST answers the question or completes the statement. *PRINT THE LETTER OF THE CORRECT ANSWER IN THE SPACE AT THE RIGHT.*

Questions 1-5.

DIRECTIONS: Questions 1 through 5 are to be answered on the basis of the Report of Offense that appears below.

REPORT OF OFFENSE   Report No. *26743*
                                                     Date of Report *10-12*

Inmate *Joseph Brown*
Age *27*   Number *61274*
Sentence *90 days*   Assignment *KU-187*
Place of offense *R.P.W., 4-1*   Date of offense *10/11/*
Offense *Assaulting inmate*
Details *During 9:00 P.M., cellblock cleanup, inmate John Jones asked for pail being used by Brown. Brown refused. Correction officer requested that Brown comply. Brown then threw pail at Jones with intent to injure him and said he would "get" Jones. Jones not hurt.*

Force used by officer *None*
Name of reporting officer *R. Rodriguez*   No. *C-2056*
Name of superior officer *P. Ferguson*

---

1. The person who made out this report is   1.____

    A. Joseph Brown   B. John Jones
    C. R. Rodriguez   D. P. Ferguson

2. Disregarding the details, the specific offense reported was   2.____

    A. insulting a fellow inmate
    B. assaulting a fellow inmate
    C. injuring a fellow inmate
    D. disobeying a correction officer

3. The number of the inmate who committed the offense is   3.____

    A. 26743   B. 61274   C. KU-187   D. C-2056

4. The offense took place on   4.____

    A. October 11   B. June 12
    C. December 10   D. November 13

5. The place where the offense occurred is identified in the report as   5.___

    A. Brown's cell   B. Jones' cell
    C. KU-187   D. R.P.W., 4-1

Questions 6-10.

DIRECTIONS: Questions 6 through 10 are to be answered on the basis of the Report of Loss or Theft that appears below.

REPORT OF LOSS OR THEFT   Date: _12/4_   Time: _9:15 A.M._

Complaint made by: _Richard Aldridge_   ❑ Owner
                306 S. Walter St.   ☒ Other - explain:
                                                  Head of Acctg. Dept.

Type of property: _Typewriter_   Value: _$'450.00_
Description: _IBM electric model #110_
Location: _768 N. Margin Ave., Accounting Dept., 3rd Floor_
Time: _Overnight 12/3 - 12/4_
Circumstances: _Mr. Aldridge reports he arrived at work 8:45 A.M., found office door open_ _and machine missing. Nothing else reported missing. I investigated and found signs of_ _forced entry; door lock was broken._
                        Signature of Reporting Officer: _B.L. Ramirez_

Notify:
   ❑ Q Building & Grounds Office, 768 N. Margin Ave.
   ❑ Q Lost Property Office, 110 Brand Ave. 0
   ☒ Security Office, 703 N. Wide Street

---

6. The person who made this complaint is   6.___

    A. a secretary   B. a security officer
    C. Richard Aldridge   D. B.L. Ramirez

7. The report concerns a typewriter that has been   7.___

    A. lost   B. damaged   C. stolen   D. sold

8. The person who took the typewriter PROBABLY entered the office through   8.___

    A. a door   B. a window
    C. the roof   D. the basement

9. When did the head of the Accounting Department FIRST notice that the typewriter was missing?   9.___

    A. December 4 at 9:15 A.M.
    B. December 4 at 8:45 A.M.
    C. The night of December 3
    D. The night of December 4

10. The event described in the report took place at   10._____

    A. 306 South Walter Street   B. 768 North Margin Avenue
    C. 110 Brand Avenue   D. 703 North Wide Street

Questions 11-15.

DIRECTIONS: Questions 11 through 15 are to be answered on the basis of the following excerpt from a recorded Annual Report of the Police Department. This material should be read first and then referred to in answering these questions, which are to be answered SOLELY on the basis of the material herein contained.

LEGAL BUREAU

One of the more important functions of this bureau is to analyze and furnish the department with pertinent information concerning Federal and State statutes and local laws which affect the department, law enforcement or crime prevention. In addition, all measures introduced in the State Legislature and the City Council, which may affect this department, are carefully reviewed by members of the Legal Bureau and, where necessary, opinions and recommendations thereon are prepared.

Another important function of this office is the prosecution of cases in the Magistrate's Courts. This is accomplished by assignment of attorneys who are members of the Legal Bureau to appear in those cases which are deemed to raise issues of importance to the department or questions of law which require technical presentation to facilitate proper determination; and also in those cases where request is made for such appearance by a magistrate, some other official of the city, or a member of the force. Attorneys are regularly assigned to prosecute all cases in the Women's Court.

Proposed legislation was prepared and sponsored for introduction in the State Legislature and, at this writing, one of these proposals has already been enacted into law and five others are presently on the Governor's desk awaiting executive action. The new law prohibits the sale or possession of a hypodermic syringe or needle by an unauthorized person. The bureau's proposals awaiting executive action pertain to: an amendment to the Code of Criminal Procedure prohibiting desk officers from taking bail in gambling cases or in cases mentioned in Section 552, Code of Criminal Procedure, including confidence men and swindlers as jostlers in the Penal Law; prohibiting the sale of switch-blade knives of any size to children under 16 and bills extending the licensing period of gunsmiths.

The Legal Bureau has regularly cooperated with the Corporation Counsel and the District Attorneys in respect to matters affecting this department, and has continued to advise and represent the Police Athletic League, the Police Sports Association, the Police Relief Fund, and the Police Pension Fund.

The following is a statistical report of the activities of the bureau during the current year as compared with the previous year:

	Current Year	Previous Year
Memoranda of law prepared	68	83
Legal matters forwarded to Corporation Counsel	122	144
Letters requesting legal information	756	807
Letters requesting departmental records	139	111
Matters for publication	17	26
Court appearances of members of bureau	4,678	4,621
Conferences	94	103
Lectures at Police Academy	30	33
Reports on proposed legislation	194	255
Deciphering of codes	79	27
Expert testimony	31	16
Notices to court witnesses	55	81
Briefs prepared	22	18
Court papers prepared	258	---

11. One of the functions of the Legal Bureau is to

11.____

    A. review and make recommendations on proposed federal laws affecting law enforcement
    B. prepare opinions on all measures introduced in the state legislature and the City Council
    C. furnish the Police Department with pertinent information concerning all new federal and state laws
    D. analyze all laws affecting the work of the Police Department

12. The Legal Bureau sponsored a bill that would

12.____

    A. extend the licenses of gunsmiths
    B. prohibit the sale of switch-blade knives to children of any size
    C. place confidence men and swindlers in the same category as jostlers in the Penal Law
    D. prohibit desk officers from admitting gamblers, confidence men, and swindlers to bail

13. From the report, it is NOT reasonable to infer that

13.____

    A. fewer bills affecting the Police Department were introduced in the current year
    B. the preparation of court papers was a new activity assumed in the current year
    C. the Code of Criminal Procedure authorizes desk officers to accept bail in certain cases
    D. the penalty for jostling and swindling is the same

14. According to the statistical report, the activity showing the GREATEST percentage of decrease in the current year compared with the previous year was

14.____

    A. matters for publication
    B. reports on proposed legislation
    C. notices to court witnesses
    D. memoranda of law prepared

15. According to the report, the percentage of bills prepared and sponsored by the Legal   15.____
    Bureau, which were passed by the State Legislature and sent to the Governor for
    approval, was
    - A. approximately 3.1%
    - B. approximately 2.6%
    - C. approximately .5%
    - D. not capable of determination from the data given

KEY (CORRECT ANSWERS)

1. C	6. C
2. B	7. C
3. B	8. A
4. A	9. B
5. D	10. B

11.	D
12.	C
13.	D
14.	A
15.	D

TEST 2

DIRECTIONS: Each question or incomplete statement is followed by several suggested answers or completions. Select the one that BEST answers the question or completes the statement. *PRINT THE LETTER OF THE CORRECT ANSWER IN THE SPACE AT THE RIGHT.*

Questions 1-2.

DIRECTIONS: Questions 1 and 2 are to be answered on the basis of the Instructions, the Bridge and Tunnel Officer's Toll Report form, and the situation given below. The questions ask how the report form should be filled in based on the Instructions and the information given in the situation.

INSTRUCTIONS

Assume that a Bridge and Tunnel Officer on duty in a toll booth must make an entry on the following report form immediately after each incident in which a vehicle driver does not pay the correct toll.

```
┌─────────────────────────────────────────────────────────────────────────┐
│           BRIDGE AND TUNNEL OFFICER'S TOLL REPORT                         │
│                                                                           │
│   Officer _____        Date _____             │
│                                                                           │
│              Type of        Toll                                          │
│     Time     Vehicle        Collected         Explanation of Entry        │
│                                                                           │
│   1. ____    _____    _____         _____          │
│   2. ____    _____    _____         _____          │
│      ____    _____    _____         _____          │
└─────────────────────────────────────────────────────────────────────────┘
```

SITUATION

John McDonald is a Bridge and Tunnel Officer assigned to toll booth 4, between the hours of 11 P.M. and 1 A.M. On this particular tour, two incidents occurred. At 11:43 P.M., a five-axle truck stopped at the toll booth and Officer McDonald collected a $2.50 toll from the driver. As the truck passed, he realized the toll should have been $3.30, and he quickly copied the vehicle's license plate number as M724HJ. At 12:34 A.M., a motorcycle went through toll lane 4 without paying the toll. The motorcycle did not have any license plate.

1. The entry which should be made on line 1 in the second column is   1.____

  A. 11:43 P.M.   B. 12:34 A.M.
  C. five-axle truck   D. motorcycle

2. The above passage does NOT provide the information necessary to fill in which of the   2.____
   following items?

  A. Officer   B. Date
  C. Line 1, Toll Collected   D. Line 2, Time

Questions 3-7.

DIRECTIONS: Questions 3 through 7 are to be answered on the basis of the Fact Situation and the Report of Inmate Injury form below. The questions ask how the report form should be filled in, based on the information given in the Fact Situation.

FACT SITUATION

Peter Miller is a Correction Officer assigned to duty in Cell-block A. His superior officer is John Doakes. Miller was on duty at 1:30 P.M. on March 21 when he heard a scream for help from Cell 12. He hurried to Cell 12 and found inmate Richard Rogers stamping out a flaming book of matches. Inmate John Jones was screaming. It seems that Jones had accidentally set fire to the entire book of matches while lighting a cigarette, and he had burned his left hand. Smoking was permitted at this hour. Miller reported the incident by phone, and Jones was escorted to the dispensary where his hand was treated at 2:00 P.M. by Dr. Albert Lorillo. Dr. Lorillo determined that Jones could return to his cellblock, but that he should be released from work for four days. The doctor scheduled a re-examination for March 22. A routine investigation of the incident was made by James Lopez. Jones confirmed to this officer that the above statement of the situation was correct.

```
REPORT OF INMATE INJURY

(1)   Name of inmate_____  (2)  Assignment _____
(3)   Number._____  (4)  Location _____
(5)   Nature of injury_____  (6)  Date _____
(7)   Details (how, when, where injury was incurred)_____
      _____
(8)   Received medical attention: date _____time _____
(9)   Treatment _____
(10)  Disposition (check one or more):
      ___(10-1) Return to housing area __(10-2) Return to duty
      ___(10-3) Work release __ days   __(10-4) Re-examine in ___ days
(11)  Employee reporting injury _____
(12)  Employee's supervisor or superior officer _____
(13)  Medical officer treating injury_____
(14)  Investigating officer _____
(15)  Head of institution _____
```

3. Which of the following should be entered in Item 1?   3._____

    A. Peter Miller   B. John Doakes
    C. Richard Rogers   D. John Jones

4. Which of the following should be entered in Item 11?   4._____

    A. Peter Miller   B. James Lopez
    C. Richard Rogers   D. John Jones

5. Which of the following should be entered in Item 8?   5._____

    A. 2/21, 1:30 P.M.   B. 2/21, 2:00 P.M.
    C. 3/21, 1:30 P.M.   D. 3/21, 2:00 P.M.

6. For Item 10, which of the following should be checked?

6.___

    A. 10-4 *only*   B. 10-1 and 10-4
    C. 10-1, 10-3, and 10-4   D. 10-2, 10-3, and 10-4

7. Of the following items, which one CANNOT be filled in on the basis of the information given in the Fact Situation? Item

7.___

    A. 12   B. 13   C. 14   D. 15

Questions 8-11.

DIRECTIONS: Questions 8 through 11 are to be answered on the basis of the Fact Situation and the Traffic Control Report form below. Read the Fact Situation carefully, and examine the blank report form. The questions ask how the report form should be filled in based on the information given in the Fact Situation.

FACT SITUATION

Mary Fields is a Traffic Control Agent. Her City Employee Number is Z90019. She is assigned to duty at the intersection of Silver Street and Amber Avenue. On the morning of May 15, she arrives at this intersection at 8:00 A.M. and sees that there is a new *patch job* on the surface of Amber Avenue in the middle of the pedestrian crosswalk and near the north-west corner of the intersection. The day before, an emergency crew was digging here. The hole is now closed and resurfaced, but the patch job on the surface was not done very well. The patch is nearly an inch higher than the surrounding surface, and it has a sharp edge that pedestrians are likely to trip on. Mary Fields thinks this condition is dangerous, and she reports it on the Traffic Control Report form.

TRAFFIC CONTROL REPORT:
DEFECTIVE EQUIPMENT OR UNSAFE CONDITION

1. Date of observation _____   2. Time _____
3. Exact location _____
4. Type of equipment or condition found to be defective or
     unsafe _____
5. Type of defect _____
6. Name of reporting Agent_____
7. Employee no. _____   8. Precinct no._____

---

8. Which of the following should be entered in Blank 3?

8.___

    A. Silver Street at Amber Avenue, near northeast corner
    B. Silver Street at Amber Avenue, near northwest corner
    C. Amber Avenue at Silver Street, near northeast corner
    D. Amber Avenue at Silver Street, near northwest corner

9. Which of the following should be entered in Blank 4?

9.___

    A. Pedestrian traffic signals
    B. Pedestrian crosswalk markings
    C. Surface patch
    D. Unsafe condition

10. The information called for in Blank 5 is needed to determine what kind of repairs must be made and what kind of repair crew must be sent.
    Which of the following entries for Blank 5 will be MOST useful to the people who receive this report in deciding what kind of repair crew to assign to the job?

    A. Pedestrians may stumble and fall.
    B. New patch is higher than rest of surface.
    C. Emergency crew dug a hole here.
    D. Street repairs were not done very well.

10._____

11. There is one blank on the form for which the Fact Situation does not provide the information needed.
    The blank that CANNOT be filled out on the basis of the information given is Blank

    A. 2   B. 6   C. 7   D. 8

11._____

Questions 12-15.

DIRECTIONS: Questions 12 through 15 are to be answered on the basis of the Fact Situation and the Report of Arrest form below. Questions ask how the report form should be filled in based on the information given in the Fact Situation.

FACT SITUATION

Jesse Stein is a special officer (security officer) who is assigned to a welfare center at 435 East Smythe Street, Brooklyn. He was on duty there Thursday morning, February 1. At 10:30 A.M., a client named Jo Ann Jones, 40 years old, arrived with her 10-year-old son Peter. Another client, Mary Alice Wiell, 45 years old, immediately began to insult Mrs. Jones. When Mrs. Jones told her to *go away,* Mrs. Wiell pulled out a long knife. The special officer (security officer) intervened and requested Mrs. Wiell to drop the knife. She would not, and he had to use necessary force to disarm her. He arrested her on charges of disorderly conduct, harassment, and possession of a dangerous weapon. Mrs. Wiell lives at 118 Healy Street, Brooklyn, Apartment 4F, and she is unemployed. The reason for her aggressive behavior is not known.

```
┌─────────────────────────────────────────────────────────────────────────┐
│ REPORT OF ARREST                                                          │
│                                                                           │
│ (01) _____    (08 _____  │
│       (Prisoner's surname) (first) (initial)            (Precinct)        │
│                                                                           │
│ (02) _____    (09 _____  │
│       (Address)                                         (Date of arrest)  │
│                                                         (Month, Day)      │
│                                                                           │
│ (03) _____ (04) _____ (05) _____                           │
│      (Date of birth)    (Age)          (Sex)      (10) _____  │
│                                                         (Time of arrest)  │
│                                                                           │
│ (06) _____ (07) _____        (11) _____  │
│      (Occupation)     (Where employed)                  (Place of arrest) │
│                                                                           │
│ (12) _____       │
│       (Specific offenses)                                                 │
│                                                                           │
│ (13) _____    (14) _____  │
│       (Arresting officer)                               (Officer's No.)   │
└─────────────────────────────────────────────────────────────────────────┘
```

12. What entry should be made in Blank 01?   12.____

    A. Jo Ann Jones   B. Jones, Jo Ann
    C. Mary Wiell   D. Wiell, Mary A.

13. Which of the following should be entered in Blank 04?   13.____

    A. 40   B. 40's
    C. 45   D. Middle-aged

14. Which of the following should be entered in Blank 09?   14.____

    A. Wednesday, February 1, 10:30 A.M.
    B. February 1
    C. Thursday morning, February 2
    D. Morning, February 4

15. Of the following, which would be the BEST entry to make in Blank 11?   15.____

    A. Really Street Welfare Center
    B. Brooklyn
    C. 435 E. Smythe St., Brooklyn
    D. 118 Heally St., Apt. 4F

KEY (CORRECT ANSWERS)

1.	C		6.	C
2.	B		7.	D
3.	D		8.	D
4.	A		9.	C
5.	D		10.	B

11.	D
12.	D
13.	C
14.	B
15.	C

———

PREPARING WRITTEN MATERIAL

PARAGRAPH REARRANGEMENT
COMMENTARY

The sentences which follow are in scrambled order. You are to rearrange them in proper order and indicate the letter choice containing the correct answer at the space at the right.

Each group of sentences in this section is actually a paragraph presented in scrambled order. Each sentence in the group has a place in that paragraph; no sentence is to be left out. You are to read each group of sentences and decide upon the best order in which to put the sentences so as to form as well-organized paragraph.

The questions in this section measure the ability to solve a problem when all the facts relevant to its solution are not given.

More specifically, certain positions of responsibility and authority require the employee to discover connections between events sometimes, apparently, unrelated. In order to do this, the employee will find it necessary to correctly infer that unspecified events have probably occurred or are likely to occur. This ability becomes especially important when action must be taken on incomplete information.

Accordingly, these questions require competitors to choose among several suggested alternatives, each of which presents a different sequential arrangement of the events. Competitors must choose the MOST logical of the suggested sequences.

In order to do so, they may be required to draw on general knowledge to infer missing concepts or events that are essential to sequencing the given events. Competitors should be careful to infer only what is essential to the sequence. The plausibility of the wrong alternatives will always require the inclusion of unlikely events or of additional chains of events which are NOT essential to sequencing the given events.

It's very important to remember that you are looking for the best of the four possible choices, and that the best choice of all may not even be one of the answers you're given to choose from.

There is no one right way to these problems. Many people have found it helpful to first write out the order of the sentences, as they would have arranged them, on their scrap paper before looking at the possible answers. If their optimum answer is there, this can save them some time. If it isn't, this method can still give insight into solving the problem. Others find it most helpful to just go through each of the possible choices, contrasting each as they go along. You should use whatever method feels comfortable, and works, for you.

While most of these types of questions are not that difficult, we've added a higher percentage of the difficult type, just to give you more practice. Usually there are only one or two questions on this section that contain such subtle distinctions that you're unable to answer confidently, and you then may find yourself stuck deciding between two possible choices, neither of which you're sure about.

———

EXAMINATION SECTION
TEST 1

DIRECTIONS: Each question consists of several sentences which can be arranged in a logical sequence. For each question, select the choice which places the numbered sentences in the MOST logical sequence. *PRINT THE LETTER OF THE CORRECT ANSWER IN THE SPACE AT THE RIGHT.*

1.   I.   A body was found in the woods.
      II.   A man proclaimed innocence.
      III. The owner of a gun was located.
      IV. A gun was traced.
      V.   The owner of a gun was questioned.
    The CORRECT answer is:

    A. IV, III, V, II, I   B. II, I, IV, III, V
    C. I, IV, III, V, II   D. I, III, V, II, IV
    E. I, II, IV, III, V

1.____

2.   I.   A man was in a hunting accident.
      II.   A man fell down a flight of steps.
      III. A man lost his vision in one eye.
      IV. A man broke his leg.
      V.   A man had to walk with a cane.
    The CORRECT answer is:

    A. II, IV, V, I, III   B. IV, V, I, III, II
    C. III, I, IV, V, II   D. I, III, V, II, IV
    E. I, III, II, IV, V

2.____

3.   I.   A man is offered a new job.
      II.   A woman is offered a new job.
      III. A man works as a waiter.
      IV. A woman works as a waitress.
      V.   A woman gives notice.
    The CORRECT answer is:

    A. IV, II, V, III, I   B. IV, II, V, I, III
    C. II, IV, V, III, I   D. III, I, IV, II, V
    E. IV, III, II, V, I

3.____

4.   I.   A train left the station late.
      II.   A man was late for work.
      III. A man lost his job.
      IV. Many people complained because the train was late.
      V.   There was a traffic jam.
    The CORRECT answer is:

    A. V, II, I, IV, III   B. V, I, IV, II, III
    C. V, I, II, IV, III   D. I, V, IV, II, III
    E. II, I, IV, V, III

4.____

5.   I.   The burden of proof as to each issue is determined before trial and remains upon the same party throughout the trial.

     II.   The jury is at liberty to believe one witness' testimony as against a number of contradictory witnesses.

     III.   In a civil case, the party bearing the burden of proof is required to prove his contention by a fair preponderance of the evidence.

     IV.   However, it must be noted that a fair preponderance of evidence does not necessarily mean a greater number of witnesses.

     V.   The burden of proof is the burden which rests upon one of the parties to an action to persuade the trier of the facts, generally the jury, that a proposition he asserts is true.

     VI.   If the evidence is equally balanced, or if it leaves the jury in such doubt as to be unable to decide the controversy either way, judgment must be given against the party upon whom the burden of proof rests.

The CORRECT answer is:

   A.   III, II, V, IV, I, VI   B.   I, II,VI,V,III,IV
   C.   III, IV, V, I, II, VI   D.   V, I, III,VI, IV, II
   E.   I,V, III, VI, IV, II

6.   I.   If a parent is without assets and is unemployed, he cannot be convicted of the crime of non-support of a child.

     II.   The term *sufficient ability* has been held to mean sufficient financial ability.

     III.   It does not matter if his unemployment is by choice or unavoidable circumstances.

     IV.   If he fails to take any steps at all, he may be liable to prosecution for endangering the welfare of a child.

     V.   Under the penal law, a parent is responsible for the support of his minor child only if the parent is *of* sufficient ability.

     VI.   An indigent parent may meet his obligation by borrowing money or by seeking aid under the provisions of the Social Welfare Law.

The CORRECT answer is:

   A.   VI, I, V, III, II, IV   B.   I, III, V, II, IV, VI
   C.   V, II, I, III, VI, IV   D.   I, VI, IV, V, II, III
   E.   II, V, I, III, VI, IV

7.   I.   Consider, for example, the case of a rabble rouser who urges a group of twenty people to go out and break the windows of a nearby factory.

     II.   Therefore, the law fills the indicated gap with the crime of *inciting to riot*.

     III.   A person is considered guilty of inciting to riot when he urges ten or more persons to engage in tumultuous and violent conduct of a kind likely to create public alarm.

     IV.   However, if he has not obtained the cooperation of at least four people, he cannot be charged with unlawful assembly.

     V.   The charge of inciting to riot was added to the law to cover types of conduct which cannot be classified as either the crime of *riot* or the crime of *unlawful assembly*.

     VI.   If he acquires the acquiescence of at least four of them, he is guilty of unlawful assembly even if the project does not materialize.

The CORRECT answer is:

A. III, V, I, VI, IV, II   B. V, I, IV, VI, II, III
C. III, IV, I, V, II, VI   D. V, I, IV, VI, III, II
E. V, III, I, VI, IV, II

8.   I.   If, however, the rebuttal evidence presents an issue of credibility, it is for the jury to   8.____
      determine whether the presumption has, in fact, been destroyed.
   II.   Once sufficient evidence to the contrary is introduced, the presumption disappears from the trial.
   III.   The effect of a presumption is to place the burden upon the adversary to come forward with evidence to rebut the presumption.
   IV.   When a presumption is overcome and ceases to exist in the case, the fact or facts which gave rise to the presumption still remain.
   V.   Whether a presumption has been overcome is ordinarily a question for the court.
   VI.   Such information may furnish a basis for a logical inference.
The CORRECT answer is:

A. IV, VI, II, V, I, III   B. III, II, V, I, IV, VI
C. V, III, VI, IV, II, I   D. V, IV, I, II, VI, III
E. II, III, V, I, IV, VI

9.   I.   An executive may answer a letter by writing his reply on the face of the letter itself   9.____
      instead of having a return letter typed.
   II.   This procedure is efficient because it saves the executive's time, the typist's time, and saves office file space.
   III.   Copying machines are used in small offices as well as large offices to save time and money in making brief replies to business letters.
   IV.   A copy is made on a copying machine to go into the company files, while the original is mailed back to the sender.
The CORRECT answer is:

A. I, II, IV, III   B. I, IV, II, III
C. III, I, IV, II   D. III, IV, II, I

10.   I.   Most organizations favor one of the types but always include the others to a lesser   10.____
      degree.
   II.   However, we can detect a definite trend toward greater use of symbolic control.
   III.   We suggest that our local police agencies are today primarily utilizing material control.
   IV.   Control can be classified into three types: physical, material, and symbolic.
The CORRECT answer is:

A. IV, II, III, I   B. II, I, IV, III
C. III, IV, II, I   D. IV, I, III, II

11.   I.   Project residents had first claim to this use, followed by surrounding neighborhood   11.____
      children.
   II.   By contrast, recreation space within the project's interior was found to be used more often by both groups.
   III.   Studies of the use of project grounds in many cities showed grounds left open for public use were neglected and unused, both by residents and by members of the surrounding community.

IV. Project residents had clearly laid claim to the play spaces, setting up and enforcing unwritten rules for use.

V. Each group, by experience, found their activities easily disrupted by other
groups, and their claim to the use of space for recreation difficult to enforce.

The CORRECT answer is:

A. IV, V, I, II, III   B. V, II, IV, III, I
C. I, IV, III, II, V   D. III, V, II, IV, I

12.   I. They do not consider the problems correctable within the existing subsidy formula 12.____
and social policy of accepting all eligible applicants regardless of social behavior
and lifestyle.

II. A recent survey, however, indicated that tenants believe these problems correctable by local housing authorities and management within the existing financial
formula.

III. Many of the problems and complaints concerning public housing management
and design have created resentment between the tenant and the landlord.

IV. This same survey indicated that administrators and managers do not agree with
the tenants.

The CORRECT answer is:

A. II, I, III, IV   B. I, III, IV, II
C. III, II, IV, I   D. IV, II, I, III

13.   I. In single-family residences, there is usually enough distance between tenants to 13.____
prevent occupants from annoying one another.

II. For example, a certain small percentage of tenant families has one or more
members addicted to alcohol.

III. While managers believe in the right of individuals to live as they choose, the
manager becomes concerned when the pattern of living jeopardizes others'
rights.

IV. Still others turn night into day, staging lusty entertainments which carry on into
the hours when most tenants are trying to sleep.

V. In apartment buildings, however, tenants live so closely together that any misbe-
havior can result in unpleasant living conditions.

VI. Other families engage in violent argument.

The CORRECT answer is:

A. III, II, V, IV, VI, I   B. I, V, II, VI, IV, III
C. II, V, IV, I, III, VI   D. IV, II, V, VI, III, I

14.   I. Congress made the commitment explicit in the Housing Act of 1949, establishing 14.____
as a national goal the realization of *a decent home and suitable environment for
every American family.*

II. The result has been that the goal of decent home and suitable environment is
still as far distant as ever for the disadvantaged urban family.

III. In spite of this action by Congress, federal housing programs have continued to
be fragmented and grossly underfunded.

IV. The passage of the National Housing Act signalled a new federal commitment to
provide housing for the nation's citizens.

The CORRECT answer is:

A. I, IV, III, II   B. IV, I, III, II
C. IV, I, II, III   D. II, IV, I, III

15.   I.   The greater expense does not necessarily involve *exploitation,* but it is often per-   15.____
            ceived as exploitative and unfair by those who are aware of the price differences
            involved, but unaware of operating costs.
      II.   Ghetto residents believe they are *exploited* by local merchants, and evidence
            substantiates some of these beliefs.
     III.   However, stores in low-income areas were more likely to be small independents,
            which could not achieve the economies available to supermarket chains and
            were, therefore, more likely to charge higher prices, and the customers were
            more likely to buy smaller-sized packages which are more expensive per unit of
            measure.
     IV.   A study conducted in one city showed that distinctly higher prices were charged
            for goods sold in ghetto stores than in other areas.
    The CORRECT answer is:

A. IV, II, I, III   B. IV, I, III, II
C. II, IV, III, I   D. II, III, IV, I

KEY (CORRECT ANSWERS)

1.	C		6.	C
2.	E		7.	A
3.	B		8.	B
4.	D		9.	C
5.	D		10.	D

11.	D
12.	C
13.	B
14.	B
15.	C

PREPARING WRITTEN MATERIAL

EXAMINATION SECTION
TEST 1

Questions 1-15.

DIRECTIONS: For each of Questions 1 through 15, select from the options given below the MOST applicable choice, and mark your answer accordingly.

    A.   The sentence is correct.
    B.   The sentence contains a spelling error *only.*
    C.   The sentence contains an English grammar error *only.*
    D.   The sentence contains both a spelling error and an English grammar error.

1.   He is a very dependible person whom we expect will be an asset to this division.   1.____

2.   An investigator often finds it necessary to be very diplomatic when conducting an inter-view.   2.____

3.   Accurate detail is especially important if court action results from an investigation.   3.____

4.   The report was signed by him and I since we conducted the investigation jointly.   4.____

5.   Upon receipt of the complaint, an inquiry was begun.   5.____

6.   An employee has to organize his time so that he can handle his workload efficiantly.   6.____

7.   It was not apparant that anyone was living at the address given by the client.   7.____

8.   According to regulations, there is to be at least three attempts made to locate the client.   8.____

9.   Neither the inmate nor the correction officer was willing to sign a formal statement.   9.____

10.   It is our opinion that one of the persons interviewed were lying.   10.____

11.   We interviewed both clients and departmental personel in the course of this investiga-tion.   11.____

12.   It is concievable that further research might produce additional evidence.   12.____

13.   There are too many occurences of this nature to ignore.   13.____

14.   We cannot accede to the candidate's request.   14.____

15.   The submission of overdue reports is the reason that there was a delay in completion of this investigation.   15.____

Questions 16-25.

DIRECTIONS: Each of Questions 16 through 25 may be classified under one of the following four categories:

    A. Faulty because of incorrect grammar or sentence structure
    B. Faulty because of incorrect punctuation
    C. Faulty because of incorrect spelling
    D. Correct

Examine each sentence carefully to determine under which of the above four options it is best classified. Then, in the space at the right, write the letter preceding the option which is the BEST of the four suggested above. Each incorrect sentence contains but one type of error. Consider a sentence to be correct if it contains none of the types of errors mentioned, even though there may be other correct ways of expressing the same thought.

16. Although the department's supply of scratch pads and stationary have diminished considerably, the allotment for our division has not been reduced.   16.___

17. You have not told us whom you wish to designate as your secretary.   17.___

18. Upon reading the minutes of the last meeting, the new proposal was taken up for consideration.   18.___

19. Before beginning the discussion, we locked the door as a precautionery measure.   19.___

20. The supervisor remarked, "Only those clerks, who perform routine work, are permitted to take a rest period."   20.___

21. Not only will this duplicating machine make accurate copies, but it will also produce a quantity of work equal to fifteen transcribing typists.   21.___

22. "Mr. Jones," said the supervisor, "we regret our inability to grant you an extention of your leave of absence."   22.___

23. Although the employees find the work monotonous and fatigueing, they rarely complain.   23.___

24. We completed the tabulation of the receipts on time despite the fact that Miss Smith our fastest operator was absent for over a week.   24.___

25. The reaction of the employees who attended the meeting, as well as the reaction of those who did not attend, indicates clearly that the schedule is satisfactory to everyone concerned.   25.___

KEY (CORRECT ANSWERS)

1.	D		11.	B
2.	A		12.	B
3.	A		13.	B
4.	C		14.	A
5.	A		15.	C
6.	B		16.	A
7.	B		17.	D
8.	C		18.	A
9.	A		19.	C
10.	C		20.	B

21.	A
22.	C
23.	C
24.	B
25.	D

———

TEST 2

Questions 1-15.

DIRECTIONS: Questions 1 through 15 consist of two sentences. Some are correct according to ordinary formal English usage. Others are incorrect because they contain errors in English usage, spelling, or punctuation. Consider a sentence correct if it contains no errors in English usage, spelling, or punctuation, even if there may be other ways of writing the sentence correctly. Mark your answer:

    A.   If only sentence I is correct
    B.   If only sentence II is correct
    C.   If sentences I and II are correct
    D.   If neither sentence I nor II is correct

1.   I.   The influence of recruitment efficiency upon administrative standards is readily apparant.   1.____
    II.   Rapid and accurate thinking are an essential quality of the police officer.

2.   I.   The administrator of a police department is constantly confronted by the demands of subordinates for increased personnel in their respective units.   2.____
    II.   Since a chief executive must work within well-defined fiscal limits, he must weigh the relative importance of various requests.

3.   I.   The two men whom the police arrested for a parking violation were wanted for robbery in three states.   3.____
    II.   Strong executive control from the top to the bottom of the enterprise is one of the basic principals of police administration.

4.   I.   When he gave testimony unfavorable to the defendant loyalty seemed to mean very little.   4.____
    II.   Having run off the road while passing a car, the patrolman gave the driver a traffic ticket.

5.   I.   The judge ruled that the defendant's conversation with his doctor was a priviliged communication.   5.____
    II.   The importance of our training program is widely recognized; however, fiscal difficulties limit the program's effectiveness.

6.   I.   Despite an increase in patrol coverage, there were less arrests for crimes against property this year.   6.____
    II.   The investigators could hardly have expected greater cooperation from the public.

7.   I.   Neither the patrolman nor the witness could identify the defendant as the driver of the car.   7.____
    II.   Each of the officers in the class received their certificates at the completion of the course.

8. I. The new commander made it clear that those kind of procedures would no longer   8.____
        be permitted.
    II. Giving some weight to performance records is more advisable then making pro-
        motions solely on the basis of test scores.

9. I. A deputy sheriff must ascertain whether the debtor, has any property.   9.____
    II. A good deputy sheriff does not cause histerical excitement when he executes a
        process.

10. I. Having learned that he has been assigned a judgment debtor, the deputy sheriff   10.____
        should call upon him.
    II. The deputy sheriff may seize and remove property without requiring a bond.

11. I. If legal procedures are not observed, the resulting contract is not enforseable.   11.____
    II. If the directions from the creditor's attorney are not in writing, the deputy sheriff
        should request a letter of instructions from the attorney.

12. I. The deputy sheriff may confer with the defendant and may enter this defendants'   12.____
        place of business.
    II. A deputy sheriff must ascertain from the creditor's attorney whether the debtor
        has any property against which he may proceede.

13. I. The sheriff has a right to do whatever is reasonably necessary for the purpose of   13.____
        executing the order of the court.
    II. The written order of the court gives the sheriff general authority and he is gov-
        erned in his acts by a very simple principal.

14. I. Either the patrolman or his sergeant are always ready to help the public.   14.____
    II. The sergeant asked the patrolman when he would finish the report.

15. I. The injured man could not hardly talk.   15.____
    II. Every officer had ought to hand in their reports on time.

Questions 16-25.

DIRECTIONS: For each of the sentences given below, numbered 16 through 25, select from
the following choices the MOST correct choice and print your choice in the
space at the right. Select as your answer:

     A. If the statement contains an unnecessary word or expression
     B. If the statement contains a slang term or expression ordinarily not
       acceptable in government report writing
     C. If the statement contains an old-fashioned word or expression, where a
       concrete, plain term would be more useful
     D. If the statement contains no major faults

16. Every one of us should try harder   16.____

17. Yours of the first instant has been received.   17.____

18. We will have to do a real snow job on him.   18.____

19. I shall contact him next Thursday.   19.____

20. None of us were invited to the meeting with the community.   20._____

21. We got this here job to do.   21._____

22. She could not help but see the mistake in the checkbook.   22._____

23. Don't bug the Director about the report.   23._____

24. I beg to inform you that your letter has been received.   24._____

25. This project is all screwed up.   25._____

———

KEY (CORRECT ANSWERS)

1.	D	11.	B
2.	C	12.	D
3.	A	13.	A
4.	D	14.	D
5.	B	15.	D
6.	B	16.	D
7.	A	17.	C
8.	D	18.	B
9.	D	19.	D
10.	C	20.	D

21.	B
22.	D
23.	B
24.	C
25.	B

———

TEST 3

DIRECTIONS: Questions 1 through 25 are sentences taken from reports. Some are correct according to ordinary formal English usage. Others are incorrect because they contain errors in English usage, spelling, or punctuation. Consider a sentence correct if it contains no errors in English usage, spelling, or punctuation, even if there may be other ways of writing the sentence correctly. Mark your answer:

    A.   If only sentence I is correct
    B.   If only sentence II is correct
    C.   If sentences I and II are correct
    D.   If neither sentence I nor II is correct.

1.   I.   The Neighborhood Police Team Commander and Team Patrol- men are encouraged to give to the public the widest possible verbal and written disemination of information regarding the existence and purposes of the program.
    II. The police must be vitally interelated with every segment of the public they serve.

                                                   1._____

2.   I.   If social gambling, prostitution, and other vices are to be prohibited, the law makers should provide the manpower and method for enforcement.
    II. In addition to checking on possible crime locations such as hallways, roofs yards and other similar locations, Team Patrolmen are encouraged to make known their presence to members of the community.

                                                   2._____

3.   I.   The Neighborhood Police Team Commander is authorized to secure, the cooperation of local publications, as well as public and private agencies, to further the goals of the program.
    II. Recruitment from social minorities is essential to effective police work among minorities and meaningful relations with them.

                                                   3._____

4.   I.   The Neighborhood Police Team Commander and his men have the responsibility for providing patrol service within the sector territory on a twenty-four hour basis.
    II. While the patrolman was walking his beat at midnight he noticed that the clothing stores' door was partly open.

                                                   4._____

5.   I.   Authority is granted to the Neighborhood Police Team to device tactics for coping with the crime in the sector.
    II. Before leaving the scene of the accident, the patrolman drew a map showing the positions of the automobiles and indicated the time of the accident as 10 M. in the morning.

                                                   5._____

6.   I.   The Neighborhood Police Team Commander and his men must be kept apprised of conditions effecting their sector.
    II. Clear, continuous communication with every segment of the public served based on the realization of mutual need and founded on trust and confidence is the basis for effective law enforcement.

                                                   6._____

7.   I.   The irony is that the police are blamed for the laws they enforce when they are   7.____
doing their duty.
       II.   The Neighborhood Police Team Commander is authorized to prepare and distribute literature with pertinent information telling the public whom to contact for assistance.

8.   I.   The day is not far distant when major parts of the entire police compliment will   8.____
need extensive college training or degrees.
       II.   Although driving under the influence of alcohol is a specific charge in making arrests, drunkeness is basically a health and social problem.

9.   I.   If a deputy sheriff finds that property he has to attach is located on a ship, he   9.____
should notify his supervisor.
       II.   Any contract that tends to interfere with the administration of justice is illegal.

10.   I.   A mandate or official order of the court to the sheriff or other officer directs it to take   10.____
into possession property of the judgment debtor.
       II.   Tenancies from month-to-month, week-to-week, and sometimes year-to-year are termenable.

11.   I.   A civil arrest is an arrest pursuant to an order issued by a court in civil litigation.   11.____
       II.   In a criminal arrest, a defendant is arrested for a crime he is alleged to have committed.

12.   I.   Having taken a defendant into custody, there is a complete restraint of personal liberty.   12.____
       II.   Actual force is unnecessary when a deputy sheriff makes an arrest.

13.   I.   When a husband breaches a separation agreement by failing to supply to the wife   13.____
the amount of money to be paid to her periodically under the agreement, the same legal steps may be taken to enforce his compliance as in any other breach of contract.
       II.   Having obtained the writ of attachment, the plaintiff is then in the advantageous position of selling the very property that has been held for him by the sheriff while he was obtaining a judgment.

14.   I.   Being locked in his desk, the investigator felt sure that the records would be safe.   14.____
       II.   The reason why the witness changed his statement was because he had been threatened.

15.   I.   The investigation had just began then an important witness disappeared.   15.____
       II.   The check that had been missing was located and returned to its owner, Harry Morgan, a resident of Suffolk County, New York.

16.   I.   A supervisor will find that the establishment of standard procedures enables his   16.____
staff to work more efficiently.
       II.   An investigator hadn't ought to give any recommendations in his report if he is in doubt.

17.   I.   Neither the investigator nor his supervisor is ready to interview the witnesses.   17.____
       II.   Interviewing has been and always will be an important asset in investigation.

18.   I.   One of the investigator's reports has been forwarded to the wrong person.   18.____
      II.   The investigator stated that he was not familiar with those kind of cases.

19.   I.   Approaching the victim of the assault, two large bruises were noticed by me.   19.____
      II.   The prisoner was arrested for assault, resisting arrest, and use of a deadly weapon.

20.   I.   A copy of the orders, which had been prepared by the captain, was given to each   20.____
          patrolman.
      II.   It's always necessary to inform an arrested person of his constitutional rights before asking him any questions.

21.   I.   To prevent further bleeding, I applied a tourniquet to the wound.   21.____
      II.   John Rano a senior officer was on duty at the time of the accident.

22.   I.   Limiting the term "property" to tangible property, in the criminal mischief setting,   22.____
          accords with prior case law holding that only tangible property came within the purview of the offense of malicious mischief.
      II.   Thus, a person who intentionally destroys the property of another, but under an honest belief that he has title to such property, cannot be convicted of criminal mischief under the Revised Penal Law.

23.   I.   Very early in it's history, New York enacted statutes from time to time punishing,   23.____
          either as a felony or as a misdemeanor, malicious injuries to various kinds of property: piers, booms, dams, bridges, etc.
      II.   The application of the statute is necessarily restricted to trespassory takings with larcenous intent: namely with intent permanently or virtually permanently to "appropriate" property or "deprive" the owner of its use.

24.   I.   Since the former Penal Law did not define the instruments of forgery in a general   24.____
          fashion, its crime of forgery was held to be narrower than the common law offense in this respect and to embrace only those instruments explicitly specified in the substantive provisions.
      II.   After entering the barn through an open door for the purpose of stealing, it was closed by the defendants.

25.   I.   The use of fire or explosives to destroy tangible property is proscribed by the crim-   25.____
          inal mischief provisions of the Revised Penal Law.
      II.   The defendant's taking of a taxicab for the immediate purpose of affecting his escape did not constitute grand larceny.

KEY (CORRECT ANSWERS)

1.	D	11.	C
2.	D	12.	B
3.	B	13.	C
4.	A	14.	D
5.	D	15.	B
6.	D	16.	A
7.	C	17.	C
8.	D	18.	A
9.	C	19.	B
10.	D	20.	C

21. A
22. C
23. B
24. A
25. A

———

TEST 4

Questions 1-4.

DIRECTIONS: Each of the two sentences in Questions 1 through 4 may be correct or may contain errors in punctuation, capitalization, or grammar. Mark your answer:

    A. If there is an error only in sentence I
    B. If there is an error only in sentence II
    C. If there is an error in both sentences I and II
    D. If both sentences are correct.

1.   I.   It is very annoying to have a pencil sharpener, which is not in working order.   1._____
     II. Patrolman Blake checked the door of Joe's Restaurant and found that the lock has been jammed.

2.   I.   When you are studying a good textbook is important.   2._____
     II. He said he would divide the money equally between you and me.

3.   I.   Since he went on the city council a year ago, one of his primary concerns has been safety in the streets.   3._____
     II. After waiting in the doorway for about 15 minutes, a black sedan appeared.

Questions 5-9.

DIRECTIONS: Each of the sentences in Questions 5 through 9 may be classified under one of the following four categories:
    A. Faulty because of incorrect grammar
    B. Faulty because of incorrect punctuation
    C. Faulty because of incorrect capitalization or incorrect spelling
    D. Correct

Examine each sentence carefully to determine under which of the above four options it is BEST classified. Then, in the space at the right, print the capitalized letter preceding the option which is the BEST of the four suggested above. Each faulty sentence contains but one type of error. Consider a sentence to be correct if it contains none of the types of errors mentioned, even though there may be other correct ways of expressing the same thought.

5. They told both he and I that the prisoner had escaped.   5._____

6. Any superior officer, who, disregards the just complaints of his subordinates, is remiss in the performance of his duty.   6._____

7. Only those members of the national organization who resided in the Middle west attended the conference in Chicago.   7._____

8. We told him to give the investigation assignment to whoever was available.   8._____

9. Please do not disappoint and embarass us by not appearing in court.   9._____

Questions 10-14.

DIRECTIONS: Each of Questions 10 through 14 consists of three sentences lettered A, B, and C. In each of these questions, one of the sentences may contain an error in grammar, sentence structure, or punctuation, or all three sentences may be correct. If one of the sentences in a question contains an error in grammar, sentence structure, or punctuation, print in the space at the right the capital letter preceding the sentence which contains the error. If all three sentences are correct, print the letter D.

10.   A.   Mr. Smith appears to be less competent than I in performing these duties.   10.___
            B.   The supervisor spoke to the employee, who had made the error, but did not reprimand him.
            C.   When he found the book lying on the table, he immediately notified the owner.

11.   A.   Being locked in the desk, we were certain that the papers would not be taken.   11.___
            B.   It wasn't I who dictated the telegram; I believe it was Eleanor.
            C.   You should interview whoever comes to the office today.

12.   A.   The clerk was instructed to set the machine on the table before summoning the manager.   12.___
            B.   He said that he was not familiar with those kind of activities.
            C.   A box of pencils, in addition to erasers and blotters, was included in the shipment of supplies.

13.   A.   The supervisor remarked, "Assigning an employee to the proper type of work is not always easy."   13.___
            B.   The employer found that each of the applicants were qualified to perform the duties of the position.
            C.   Any competent student is permitted to take this course if he obtains the consent of the instructor.

14.   A.   The prize was awarded to the employee whom the judges believed to be most deserving.   14.___
            B.   Since the instructor believes this book is the better of the two, he is recommending it for use in the school.
            C.   It was obvious to the employees that the completion of the task by the scheduled date would require their working overtime.

Questions 15-21.

DIRECTIONS: In answering Questions 15 through 21, choose the sentence which is BEST from the point of view of English usage suitable for a business report.

15.   A.   The client's receiving of public assistance checks at two different addresses were   15.____
disclosed by the investigation.
       B.   The investigation disclosed that the client was receiving public assistance
checks at two different addresses.
       C.   The client was found out by the investigation to be receiving public assistance
checks at two different addresses.
       D.   The client has been receiving public assistance checks at two different
addresses, disclosed the investigation.

16.   A.   The investigation of complaints are usually handled by this unit, which deals with   16.____
internal security problems in the department.
       B.   This unit deals with internal security problems in the department usually investi-
gating complaints.
       C.   Investigating complaints is this unit's job, being that it handles internal security
problems in the department.
       D.   This unit deals with internal security problems in the department and usually
investigates complaints.

17.   A.   The delay in completing this investigation was caused by difficulty in obtaining the   17.____
required documents from the candidate.
       B.   Because of difficulty in obtaining the required documents from the candidate is
the reason that there was a delay in completing this investigation.
       C.   Having had difficulty in obtaining the required documents from the candidate,
there was a delay in completing this investigation.
       D.   Difficulty in obtaining the required documents from the candidate had the affect
of delaying the completion of this investigation.

18.   A.   This report, together with documents supporting our recommendation, are being   18.____
submitted for your approval.
       B.   Documents supporting our recommendation is being submitted with the report
for your approval.
       C.   This report, together with documents supporting our recommendation, is being
submitted for your approval.
       D.   The report and documents supporting our recommendation is being submitted
for your approval.

19.   A.   The chairman himself, rather than his aides, has reviewed the report.   19.____
       B.   The chairman himself, rather than his aides, have reviewed the report.
       C.   The chairmen, not the aide, has reviewed the report.
       D.   The aide, not the chairmen, have reviewed the report.

20.   A.   Various proposals were submitted but the decision is not been made.   20.____
       B.   Various proposals has been submitted but the decision has not been made.
       C.   Various proposals were submitted but the decision is not been made.
       D.   Various proposals have been submitted but the decision has not been made.

21.   A.   Everyone were rewarded for his successful attempt.   21.____
       B.   They were successful in their attempts and each of them was rewarded.
       C.   Each of them are rewarded for their successful attempts.
       D.   The reward for their successful attempts were made to each of them.

22. The following is a paragraph from a request for departmental recognition consisting of   22._____
five numbered sentences submitted to a Captain for review. These sentences may or
may not have errors in spelling, grammar, and punctuation:

1. The officers observed the subject Mills surreptitiously remove a wallet from the
woman's handbag and entered his automobile. 2. As they approached Mills, he looked in
their direction and drove away. 3. The officers pursued in their car. 4. Mills executed a
series of complicated manuvers to evade the pursuing officers. 5. At the corner of
Broome and Elizabeth Streets, Mills stopped the car, got out, raised his hands and sur-
rendered to the officers.

Which one of the following BEST classifies the above with regard to spelling, grammar
and punctuation?

  A. 1, 2, and 3 are correct, but 4 and 5 have errors.
  B. 2, 3, and 5 are correct, but 1 and 4 have errors.
  C. 3, 4, and 5 are correct, but 1 and 2 have errors.
  D. 1, 2, 3, and 5 are correct, but 4 has errors.

23. The one of the following sentences which is grammatically PREFERABLE to the others   23._____
is:

  A. Our engineers will go over your blueprints so that you may have no problems in
    construction.
  B. For a long time he had been arguing that we, not he, are to blame for the confu-
    sion.
  C. I worked on this automobile for two hours and still cannot find out what is wrong
    with it.
  D. Accustomed to all kinds of hardships, fatigue seldom bothers veteran policemen.

24. The MOST accurate of the following sentences is: 24._____

  A. The commissioner, as well as his deputy and various bureau heads, were present.
  B. A new organization of employers and employees have been formed.
  C. One or the other of these men have been selected.
  D. The number of pages in the book is enough to discourage a reader.

25. The MOST accurate of the following sentences is: 25._____

  A. Between you and me, I think he is the better man.
  B. He was believed to be me.
  C. Is it us that you wish to see?
  D. The winners are him and her.

———

KEY (CORRECT ANSWERS)

1.	C		11.	A
2.	A		12.	B
3.	C		13.	B
4.	B		14.	D
5.	A		15.	B
6.	B		16.	D
7.	C		17.	A
8.	D		18.	C
9.	C		19.	A
10.	B		20.	D

21.	B
22.	B
23.	A
24.	D
25.	A

———

ANSWER SHEET

EST NO. _____ PART _____ TITLE OF POSITION _____

(AS GIVEN IN EXAMINATION ANNOUNCEMENT - INCLUDE OPTION, IF ANY)

PLACE OF EXAMINATION _____

(CITY OR TOWN)　　　　　(STATE)　　DATE ____

RATING

USE THE SPECIAL PENCIL.　MAKE GLOSSY BLACK MARKS.

1　2　3　4　5　6　7　8　9　10

26　27　28　29　30　31　32　33　34　35

51　52　53　54　55　56　57　58　59　60

76　77　78　79　80　81　82　83　84　85

101　102　103　104　105　106　107　108　109　110

Make only ONE mark for each answer.　Additional and stray marks may be counted as mistakes.　In making corrections, erase errors COMPLETELY.

11　12　13　14　15　16　17　18　19　20　21　22　23　24　25

36　37　38　39　40　41　42　43　44　45　46　47　48　49　50

61　62　63　64　65　66　67　68　69　70　71　72　73　74　75

86　87　88　89　90　91　92　93　94　95　96　97　98　99　100

111　112　113　114　115　116　117　118　119　120　121　122　123　124　125

ANSWER SHEET

AUG – – 2016

TEST NO. _____ PART _____ TITLE OF POSITION _____

(AS GIVEN IN EXAMINATION ANNOUNCEMENT - INCLUDE OPTION, IF ANY)

PLACE OF EXAMINATION _____ DATE_____
(CITY OR TOWN)   (STATE)

RATING

USE THE SPECIAL PENCIL.   MAKE GLOSSY BLACK MARKS.

	A B C D E		A B C D E		A B C D E		A B C D E		A B C D E
1	:: :: :: :: ::	26	:: :: :: :: ::	51	:: :: :: :: ::	76	:: :: :: :: ::	101	:: :: :: :: ::
2	:: :: :: :: ::	27	:: :: :: :: ::	52	:: :: :: :: ::	77	:: :: :: :: ::	102	:: :: :: :: ::
3	:: :: :: :: ::	28	:: :: :: :: ::	53	:: :: :: :: ::	78	:: :: :: :: ::	103	:: :: :: :: ::
4	:: :: :: :: ::	29	:: :: :: :: ::	54	:: :: :: :: ::	79	:: :: :: :: ::	104	:: :: :: :: ::
5	:: :: :: :: ::	30	:: :: :: :: ::	55	:: :: :: :: ::	80	:: :: :: :: ::	105	:: :: :: :: ::
6	:: :: :: :: ::	31	:: :: :: :: ::	56	:: :: :: :: ::	81	:: :: :: :: ::	106	:: :: :: :: ::
7	:: :: :: :: ::	32	:: :: :: :: ::	57	:: :: :: :: ::	82	:: :: :: :: ::	107	:: :: :: :: ::
8	:: :: :: :: ::	33	:: :: :: :: ::	58	:: :: :: :: ::	83	:: :: :: :: ::	108	:: :: :: :: ::
9	:: :: :: :: ::	34	:: :: :: :: ::	59	:: :: :: :: ::	84	:: :: :: :: ::	109	:: :: :: :: ::
10	:: :: :: :: ::	35	:: :: :: :: ::	60	:: :: :: :: ::	85	:: :: :: :: ::	110	:: :: :: :: ::

Make only ONE mark for each answer.   Additional and stray marks may be
counted as mistakes.   In making corrections, erase errors COMPLETELY.

	A B C D E		A B C D E		A B C D E		A B C D E		A B C D E
11	:: :: :: :: ::	36	:: :: :: :: ::	61	:: :: :: :: ::	86	:: :: :: :: ::	111	:: :: :: :: ::
12	:: :: :: :: ::	37	:: :: :: :: ::	62	:: :: :: :: ::	87	:: :: :: :: ::	112	:: :: :: :: ::
13	:: :: :: :: ::	38	:: :: :: :: ::	63	:: :: :: :: ::	88	:: :: :: :: ::	113	:: :: :: :: ::
14	:: :: :: :: ::	39	:: :: :: :: ::	64	:: :: :: :: ::	89	:: :: :: :: ::	114	:: :: :: :: ::
15	:: :: :: :: ::	40	:: :: :: :: ::	65	:: :: :: :: ::	90	:: :: :: :: ::	115	:: :: :: :: ::
16	:: :: :: :: ::	41	:: :: :: :: ::	66	:: :: :: :: ::	91	:: :: :: :: ::	116	:: :: :: :: ::
17	:: :: :: :: ::	42	:: :: :: :: ::	67	:: :: :: :: ::	92	:: :: :: :: ::	117	:: :: :: :: ::
18	:: :: :: :: ::	43	:: :: :: :: ::	68	:: :: :: :: ::	93	:: :: :: :: ::	118	:: :: :: :: ::
19	:: :: :: :: ::	44	:: :: :: :: ::	69	:: :: :: :: ::	94	:: :: :: :: ::	119	:: :: :: :: ::
20	:: :: :: :: ::	45	:: :: :: :: ::	70	:: :: :: :: ::	95	:: :: :: :: ::	120	:: :: :: :: ::
21	:: :: :: :: ::	46	:: :: :: :: ::	71	:: :: :: :: ::	96	:: :: :: :: ::	121	:: :: :: :: ::
22	:: :: :: :: ::	47	:: :: :: :: ::	72	:: :: :: :: ::	97	:: :: :: :: ::	122	:: :: :: :: ::
23	:: :: :: :: ::	48	:: :: :: :: ::	73	:: :: :: :: ::	98	:: :: :: :: ::	123	:: :: :: :: ::
24	:: :: :: :: ::	49	:: :: :: :: ::	74	:: :: :: :: ::	99	:: :: :: :: ::	124	:: :: :: :: ::
25	:: :: :: :: ::	50	:: :: :: :: ::	75	:: :: :: :: ::	100	:: :: :: :: ::	125	:: :: :: :: ::